THE ATTENDANCE ALLOWANCE AND THE COSTS OF CARING

CHRISTINE HORTON and RICHARD BERTHOUD

Policy Studies Institute

PSI Publications are obtainable from all good bookshops, or by visiting the Institute at 100 Park Village East, London NW1 3SR (071-387 2171).

Sales Representation: Pinter Publishers Ltd.

Individual and Bookshop orders to: Marston Book Services Ltd, PO Box 87, Oxford, OX4 1LB.

A CIP catalogue record of this book is available from the British Library.

OP 49

ISBN 0 85374 474 2

1000147076
0853744610

Typeset by Policy Studies Institute

Printed in Great Britain by Billing and Sons Limited, Worcester

Contents

Preface

This study of people with disabilities who receive the attendance allowance was supported by the Joseph Rowntree Memorial Trust. It was seen as a preliminary to a larger programme of research on the economic problems of disabled people also sponsored by the Trust.

Christine Horton was responsible for the fieldwork among the main sample of 'ordinary' attendance allowance claimants; Teresa Hinton interviewed members of the Bexley Community Care Scheme.

The Department of Social Security contributed to the research by selecting a sample of claimants of the attendance allowance. We are especially grateful to Nan Maitland, Community Care Manager at the London Borough of Bexley, who originally suggested the study, and who introduced us to members of the Community Care Scheme.

Warm thanks to the 38 disabled men and women, and their carers, whose willingness to discuss their lives and problems with the researchers made this study possible.

Introduction

'Community care'

About 2.3 million people in Great Britain suffer from a disability which means that they cannot look after themselves in the normal way.[1] They need 'care'.

Many live in residential care homes; some of those with the most serious problems in nursing homes. The care provided in these homes is paid for in a variety of ways: by local authorities, out of social security benefits, by the residents using their own resources, or by their relatives. There was a huge increase in the use of social security benefits to pay for residential care during the 1980s: the number of people involved rose from 13,000 in 1980 to 147,000 in 1988.[2] Some of the increase represents people who would have come into residential care anyway, and the Department of Social Security is paying bills which would otherwise have been met by someone else. But many people might not have been in a residential home at all if they had not been able to claim social security benefits to cover the fees.

While there is little doubt that the people in these homes need care,[3] this increase in support for residential care is in direct contrast to the government's declared preference for 'community care'. It is widely accepted that many people with disabilities could lead a fuller life if they were able to live at home, and receive care there. For most disabled people, care at home also costs the government less: this is a strong attraction for the keepers of the public purse, though the argument is naturally less impressive for those who may have to bear the costs of caring more directly.

Most care in the community is provided by relatives. But local authority social services departments have placed an increasing emphasis on provision for people with disabilities living in the community. Sometimes these services are provided to disabled people living alone without an informal carer; sometimes they are used to support relatives who cannot cope on their own. Caring and support services can also be provided by voluntary organisations, or by neighbours on a voluntary basis. Alternatively, disabled people or their relatives can pay an agency or an individual to help them.

The huge increase in social security payments to cover the costs of residential care has raised the question whether the same money might not be spent more effectively on care in the community. A series of official reports has examined the procedures by which public money should be made available to meet the costs of care. The most important of these, the Griffiths Report,[4] recommended that all the public resources currently available should be placed in the hands of a single agency – the local authority social services department – which would decide how much was needed by each client, and how it should be spent. A rational choice between residential and community care could be taken only if the same organisation was responsible both for assessing need and for paying the bills, whatever the decision. According to the Griffiths model, local authorities would become managers rather than providers of care services, while social security benefits would return to their original role of meeting basic living expenses.

The idea of a budget available to be spent as appropriate on the particular needs of the individual opens out a wide range of possibilities. Should the money be spent on a place in a residential home? Or should it be spent on services such as home helps, meals on wheels, day care centres or care assistants, bought-in on contract from organisations which specialise in the provision of such services? Or should an individual be paid a salary to look after the disabled person; or a team of people working a rota? One use of the money would be to allow a relative to give up work in order to concentrate on caring. A combination of these approaches might turn out to be the best package.

The Griffiths Report envisaged that when a significant amount of resources was required, the care budget would be placed in the hands of a 'care manager' – a social worker or other public servant. An alternative approach would be to hand the money direct to the disabled person, or to his or her family, to spend as they think best. This might be attractive to those who see consumer choice in a free market as the best way to ensure the efficient use of resources. On the other hand, it is not clear whether the money would be spent on care, or on other important needs such as food, fuel or clothing.

Severely disabled people in need of care already receive a social security benefit – the attendance allowance – which they are free to spend on caring services, or on other things, as they choose. This report is based on interviews with 38 claimants, designed to find out how they used their attendance allowance, and what difference, if any, it made to their arrangements for care.

The attendance allowance

The attendance allowance was introduced in 1971 as a benefit paid to people with disabilities who cannot be left on their own for long periods. It is payable to adults, and to children over the age of two, who require either frequent attention in connection with their bodily functions, or supervision to avoid substantial danger to themselves or others. Payment can start six months after the onset of the condition which qualifies the individual for attendance allowance.

The benefit is paid at two rates, according to whether the person requires attendance just during the day or just during the night (lower rate), or during both day and night (higher rate). For the year between April 1988 and March 1989, during which most of the fieldwork for this study was carried out, the two weekly rates were £22.00 and £32.95. The current rates (from April 1990) are £25.05 and £37.55.

In 1971 54,000 people received attendance allowance, whereas in 1988 it was received by thirteen times as many: 425,000 at the lower rate, 287,000 at the higher rate.[5] As the figures below show, many claimants are very old, but the benefit is nevertheless important to disabled people of working age, and children.[5]

Aged	2 to 15	71,000
	16 to 59	193,000
	60 to 74	153,000
	75 or more	337,000

The OPCS report on the financial circumstances of disabled adults confirms that the attendance allowance tends to go to those with the severest disabilities.[6] Using a 'severity' scale from one (lowest) to ten,

3

it was found that those receiving attendance allowance were concentrated in categories nine and ten. Thus 54 per cent of adults in category nine received attendance allowance and 74 per cent of those in category ten, whereas none of those in category one received the allowance.

An important feature of the attendance allowance is that entitlement depends on need and nothing else. Unlike income support, the benefit is not means-tested; indeed it is not regarded as income for the purposes of calculating income support. Neither is the benefit taxable. It therefore provides a genuine increase in resources for people receiving it. Unlike the invalidity pension or invalid care allowance, it does not depend on either the claimant or the carer being unable to work, and it is therefore not an earnings replacement benefit. The allowance does not have to be spent on care; indeed in principle it is payable even if the claimant does not receive the attendance which qualified him or her for the benefit.

It has never been clearly stated what the attendance allowance was for. A common assumption is that it was designed as a payment towards the costs of care. An alternative assumption is that it was intended to pay for the extra expenditures faced by many people with disabilities, and that the attendance criterion is simply used as an indicator of the extent of disability.

Whatever governments may have intended, another question is what the attendance allowance is spent on in practice. Social Policy Research Unit studies of families with severely disabled children have suggested that the attendance allowance tended to go towards general living expenses and/or specific items like hospital visits or compensatory 'treats', rather than on care services.[7] A National Institute for Social Work study of elderly people suffering from dementia[8] also touched on the question, and found the allowance being used in a variety of ways to cover the extra expenses which arose from the person's illness; in some cases this included services such as domestic help and 'sitting'.

Other social security benefits

The majority of people with disabilities rely on social security benefits for most of their income.[6] These are usually classified either as 'income maintenance' benefits or as 'additional costs' benefits.

Income maintenance is provided both through benefits especially for disabled people, and through mainstream social security benefits.

- The *state pension* or *invalidity benefit* are part of the national insurance scheme.
- A *disablement pension* is available to people whose disability was caused by an industrial accident or disease.
- People without an entitlement under national insurance can claim the *severe disability allowance*, paid at only 60 per cent of the rate of the contribution-based benefits.
- Those whose benefits or other income are insufficient for their basic needs can claim *income support* – formerly supplementary benefit – and *housing benefit*.

All these benefits are designed to provide claimants with the ordinary necessities of life; apart from housing benefit, they are available only to people who are not able to earn their own living.

Three benefits are designed to provide for the additional costs faced by people with disabilities.

- The *attendance allowance* has just been described.
- *Mobility allowance* is available to people who are unable or virtually unable to walk; it is explicitly intended to help them with the additional costs of transport.
- People with disabilities who claim income support or housing benefit can receive a *disability premium* which allows their minimum needs to be assessed at a higher rate than that of other claimants.

It is open to question whether the attendance allowance is designed to meet the costs of care or not. But other social security benefits are more explicitly aimed at care.

- Income support will meet the *fees of residential care or nursing homes*, up to certain limits, if the claimant's own income does not cover them; this arrangement will, however, be phased out as the responsibility is transferred to social services departments over the next few years.
- Other benefits provide income maintenance for informal carers who are prevented from working. The *invalid care allowance* is solely for that purpose, but carers can also claim *income support* if their other resources are inadequate. An

income support *carers' premium* will be introduced in October 1990.

• Under the old supplementary benefit scheme it was possible to claim extra money to pay for privately provided *domestic assistance*. Additions of this sort have been replaced by the disability premium mentioned above, but the government has also set up an *Independent Living Fund* which can meet the costs of domestic assistance and other care. This scheme, which did not exist when our research was being planned, can play an important role in meeting the costs of care for a few thousand people with disabilities, though its future will be reviewed as other aspects of community care policy develop.

The Bexley Community Care Scheme
Although there is no national policy on the use of social security benefits to pay for care at home, several local schemes have been set up to employ 'paid carers' for people with disabilities. One is the Community Care Scheme which has been operated in the London Borough of Bexley since 1984. The scheme aims to develop alternatives to residential care for elderly people suffering from multiple disabilities. The scheme currently has 60 clients, most of whom suffer senile dementia. It was inspired in part by the Kent Community Care Project which had carried out pioneering work in supporting frail elderly people in the community.

The scheme seeks to arrange packages of care tailored to an individual's needs through coordinating the contributions of public agencies, relatives and paid carers. Each client has a case manager who organises the programme of care arrangements.

Much of the money to pay for carers is provided by social security benefits. Assuming that basic benefits such as the state pension, invalidity benefit or income support are designed to meet ordinary living expenses, the case manager ensures that the client has claimed the attendance allowance at the appropriate rate. Until April 1988, the domestic assistance addition to supplementary benefit was of great value to the scheme. Since then, many of the scheme's members have successfully applied for support from the Independent Living Fund.

Members of the scheme are people who were at risk of going into residential care, but wished to remain in the community. A different package is arranged to suit each case: carers may be individually recruited paid neighbours, private agency carers, care attendants or home sharers; their services are sometimes combined with statutory services such as home helps, meals on wheels, bath attendants and district nurses.

Every member of the scheme has a 'key carer' who takes the overall responsibility for ensuring that the elderly person's needs are met. But no-one is expected to take on the whole of the task without regular help from others. Sometimes the 'key carer' is a close relative of the disabled person, but in the majority of cases no relative is available to take on the task, and the 'team' is led by a paid key carer.

A clinical psychologist is available to assess the needs of the client in terms of therapy as well as care. The scheme is run by three care managers, who put the packages of money and carers together in collaboration with relatives, statutory services and other interested parties. These packages are described in Chapter 4.

Aims of the research

This study examines the financial circumstances and care arrangements of 29 'ordinary' claimants of the attendance allowance, plus 9 members of the Bexley Community Care Scheme. The research was designed to find out what role, if any, the attendance allowance played in bringing together the package of care suited to each individual, and about the actual or potential role of paid carers in support of, or as substitutes for, kin carers.

This was an exploratory survey of a specific question about the link between one benefit and one form of care. It aims to add one or two pieces to a jigsaw, large areas of which have already been filled in by other studies.

- A series of surveys of people with disabilities conducted by the Office of Population Censuses and Surveys has provided a definitive analysis of the *prevalence of disability*,[9] analysed by the cause, nature and severity of the handicap. The same surveys offer a wealth of information about disabled people's *financial circumstances*,[6] *use of services*[1] and so on.
- A large volume of research on *informal carers* has been undertaken during the 1980s. Recent major studies include those by Janet Finch[10] and by Hazel Qureshi and Alan Walker;[11] a full review of this literature has been undertaken

7

by Gillian Parker.[12] Caroline Glendinning[13] has studied the financial costs of caring, and the views of carers.

- There has been much less research about *paid carers*, but Diana Leat[14] has looked at a variety of ways in which 'ordinary people' are paid, usually by the local authority social services department, to care for people in need. Much of her interest has been in the motivations and rewards of the paid carers; our own study tends to look at paid care more from the point of view of the disabled person, and/or their family.

- A number of other local *community care schemes* have been evaluated, notably that in Kent.[15] We should emphasise that our own look at the scheme in Bexley is intended simply to cast further light on the link between benefits and care, and is *not* an evaluation of the care provided by the scheme. This report analyses the number of hours of care delivered, and its cost, but a much more intensive enquiry would have been required to compare the quality of the care received with that available from other sources.

- The experience of claiming the *attendance allowance* has been examined in a recent report by Judith Buckle,[16] but she did not look at way in which it was spent.

- Although our particular interest is in the relationship, if any, between the attendance allowance and care, an alternative use of the benefit is to meet the *additional costs of disability*, including special diets, extra fuel or laundry costs, and so on. The OPCS surveys, mentioned above,[6] estimated these on the basis of a set questionnaire, but the Disablement Income Group has published much higher estimates based on more intensive questioning.[17] Sally Baldwin used a direct comparison of expenditure patterns to estimate these costs for children with disabilities,[7] and a similar analysis for adults is currently being undertaken by the Department of Social Security.

The research is intended to contribute to the development of two important areas of government policy, both of which are currently under consideration. One is concerned with the development of care in the community; the other is concerned with the reform of disability benefits.

The government's policy on community care has been under review since 1984. The Griffiths report, recommending the allocation of all responsibility to local authority social services departments was published in March 1988.[4] The government announced its broad acceptance of the proposals in July 1989, and published a detailed white paper in November.[18] The new policy is intended to be implemented in 1991.

When the Government announced major reforms of the structure of the main social security system, it said that decisions about benefits for people with disabilities would be made when the results of a series of major surveys of disability, carried out by the Office of Population Censuses and Surveys, were known. The reports on those surveys have now been published. In addition, the Social Security Advisory Committee, which advises the Government on social security matters, published its recommendations about how the system of benefits for disabled people should be changed. [19] The government's plans for disability benefits[20] were announced in January 1990 – after this research had been completed. Among other changes, it proposes to introduce a new 'disability allowance' incorporating the current attendance and mobility allowances, but adding a new, lower, rate of payment for people who do not qualify at present.

Research methods
The Department of Social Security supported the study by selecting a sample of attendance allowance claimants. This will be referred to as the 'main sample'. The Department selected 40 cases at random. Half received benefit at the higher rate (requiring attendance both by day and by night); the other half at the lower rate (either by day, or by night, but not both). Within each category, half of the claimants selected were adults of working age (18 to 59); the other half over pension age (65 or more).

The DSS used information about the Post Office where the benefit was cashed to confine the sample to two areas: a district of North London overlapping the Boroughs of Haringey, Islington and Hackney; and a district of Southeast London approximating to the Borough of Bexley.

The Department wrote to each of the 40 claimants informing them of the proposed study, explaining its purpose, and giving them the opportunity to have their name and address removed from the list.

Seven of the claimants were deleted by the DSS after responses to this letter: three had died, three did not wish to take part and one could not be traced. A researcher then visited each of the remaining claimants in their homes to carry out an interview. Three more declined to do so at this stage, two of them because of language difficulties. One of the claimants who gave an interview had already moved into residential care, and his circumstances were not relevant to the enquiry.

29 of the original 40 claimants therefore contributed to the study. Two of them had been reassessed for the attendance allowance, by the time they were interviewed, and had been told that they no longer fulfilled the conditions of eligibility. These two cases may not strictly fit into the sample, but information about them has been referred to in this report where it has seemed relevant.

The aim was to interview the disabled person, the main carer, and preferably both. The interviews were carried out in one or other of their homes, and frequently both individuals were interviewed together. Some of the claimants was physically unable to communicate, or were prevented through mental ill-health from carrying out a full interview, and in these cases only the main carer was interviewed. Most interviews were recorded on tape and afterwards transcribed; where the respondent asked for the tape recorder not to be used, the researcher took detailed notes.

Originally it was intended (with the permission of the disabled person) to interview the social worker dealing with each individual's case, so that we could get a clear measure of the role of formal services in support of informal carers. In the event only seven of the 29 respondents in the sample of 'ordinary' allowance claimants had an individual social worker who regularly dealt with their needs. Instead, representatives of the social services departments of each of the boroughs where the research was carried out were interviewed about the services offered to disabled people, without going into the details of particular cases.

Nine members of the Bexley Community Care Scheme were selected, and their agreement (or that of their main carer) to participate in the study obtained, with the assistance of Bexley Social Services Department. All the individuals in this sample were suffering from some form of mental ill-health or dementia, and interviews were carried out with their main carer and, in some cases, either a second carer or a close relative. The files relating to each case were consulted, and the Community Care Manager was interviewed about each case.

Table 1 provides some basic information about the members of the two groups of respondents. Although some members of the main sample of ordinary attendance allowance claimants lived in the same borough, the word 'Bexley' is always associated with members of the Community Care Scheme whenever it is used in this report.

Table 1   Details of the samples

	'Ordinary' claimants	Bexley clients
Age		
18 to 34	5	nil
35 to 60	11	nil
65 or over	13	9
Sex		
Man	7	2
Woman	22	7
Location		
North London	22	nil
South East London	7	9
Condition		
Mental handicap	5	nil
Mental illness	6	9
Physical disability only	18	nil
Rate of allowance		
Lower	14	4
Higher	15	5

The Bexley clients were very similar to each other: all were over pension age, and all suffered from senile dementia. Some of the main sample were also old, and also suffered from senile dementia or other conditions which affected their ability to take decisions for themselves. But the main sample was broader, including five young adults with mental handicaps, and many people with disabilities which required physical assistance, but who could take their own decisions about income, expenditure and care.

On the other hand, the samples had two things in common: all members of both samples received the attendance allowance, and they all needed care. Although their particular needs were often different, each sample could throw some light on the main question facing the research, about the relationship between the attendance allowance and the costs of caring.

The research was based on extremely small samples in two areas of London, and it is not possible to draw general conclusions with any confidence. The objective of the study was simply to explore the issues surrounding the use of social security benefits to pay for care, on the basis of a small number of examples. A larger scale and more structured enquiry would be needed to provide an accurate measure of the patterns which seemed to emerge.

Plan of this report
The next chapter describes the care received by members of the main sample of ordinary attendance allowance claimants, either from their family, or from other sources. We concentrate in particular on arrangements which did not fit into the standard patterns described by other studies, and on the relationship between primary carers and alternative sources of support.

Chapter 2 describes the main sample's sources of income. One focus is on the impact of the attendance allowance on a household's total resources; another is on the incomes of carers.

Chapter 3 concentrates on expenditure. It is here that the first two chapters' analyses of care and cash are linked, in an attempt to assess the impact of one upon the other.

The sample of clients of the Bexley Community Care Scheme is analysed in Chapter 4. Some of the care arrangements are described in detail, and it is possible to trace a much more direct link between the costs of caring and sources of income than could be found in the main sample.

The concluding chapter includes a summary of the findings, and a preliminary discussion of possible relationships between social security benefits and paid care.

All quotations are taken from the transcripts of tape-recorded interviews. To preserve the anonymity of the thirty-eight disabled people and their carers who took part in this study, fictitious names have been used throughout.

References

1. J. Martin, A. White, H. Meltzer, *Disabled adults: services, transport and employment*, HMSO, 1989.

2. *Commons Hansard*, vol.144, 21 December 1988, written answers, cols 303-306.

3. J. Bradshaw and I. Gibbs, *Public Support for Private Residential Care*, Avebury, 1988.

4. Sir R. Griffiths, *Community Care: agenda for action*, HMSO, 1988.

5. Department of Social Security, *Social Security Statistics, 1989*, HMSO, 1989.

6. J. Martin and A. White, *The Financial Circumstances of Disabled Adults Living in Private Households*, HMSO, 1988.

7. S. Baldwin, *The Cost of Caring*, Routledge and Kegan Paul, 1985.

8. E. Levin, I. Sinclair and P. Gorbach, *The Supporters of Confused Elderly People at Home*, National Institute of Social Work, 1983.

9. J. Martin, H. Meltzer and D. Elliot, *The Prevalence of Disability among Adults*, HMSO, 1988.

10. J. Finch, *Family Obligations and Social Change*, Polity Press, 1989.

11. H. Qureshi and A. Walker, *The Caring Relationship*, Macmillan, 1989.

12. G. Parker, *With Due Care and Attention* (2nd edition), Family Policy Studies Centre, 1990.

13. C. Glendinning, *The Financial Needs and Circumstances of Informal Carers*, Social Policy Research Unit, University of York, 1989; see also M. Nissel, and L. Bonnerjea, *Family Care of the Handicapped Elderly: who pays?*, PSI, 1982.

14. D. Leat, *Paying for Care*, PSI, 1987; *For Love and Money*, Joseph Rowntree Memorial Trust, forthcoming, 1990.

15. B. Davies and D. Challis, *Matching Resources to Needs in Community Care*, Gower, 1986; D. Challis and B. Davies, *Case Management in Community Care*, Gower, 1986; H. Qureshi, D. Challis and B. Davies, *Helpers in Case-managed Community Care*, Gower, 1989.

16. J. Buckle, *Am I Entitled?*, Disablement Income Group, 1988.

17. P. Thompson, *Short Changed by Disability*, Disablement Income Group, 1990.

18. Department of Health, *Caring for People*, HMSO, 1989.

19. Social Security Advisory Committee, *Benefits for Disabled People: a strategy for change*, HMSO, 1988.

20. Department of Social Security, *The Way Ahead: benefits for disabled people*, HMSO, 1990.

1 Carers and helpers

Primary carers

All of the disabled people we spoke to had someone on whom they could rely for the care they needed. It is sometimes useful to distinguish between the person who had accepted the responsibility for seeing that the care was provided, and someone who actually did the caring. In the majority of cases, the same person did both: that is, the person to whom the responsibility fell cared for the disabled person him or herself. On the other hand, as will be seen, some did part of the work themselves and arranged for other people to contribute. Another option could be to make the arrangements for, and supervise, a scheme of care provided by third parties. Some people with disabilities whose handicap was purely physical were able to take the role of care organiser themselves.

There has been a substantial body of research describing the extent of care provided by relatives at different degrees of kinship.[1] For our own purposes, it will be sufficient to describe the cases whose arrangements fell into standard categories, as background to the analysis of the more unusual packages which are of particular interest.

A number of authors[2] have suggested that the choice of carer follows a 'hierarchy'. Some disabled people have a single relation who will almost certainly care for them if necessary. Only if there is no-one available in that front rank might the job fall to a member of the second rank; here there might be several different relatives, and it is not clear in advance which of them, if any, will provide care. A third rank consist of people who would not normally be expected to offer care, but who might in certain circumstances. It is clear that at one end of the hierarchy people feel an obligation to care; at the other end, the role is voluntary. Another distinction between the opposite ends of the hierarchy is that the front rank often provides full-time care, whereas the third rank is more likely to contribute part-time or occasional help. In more detail, the hierarchy appears to be as follows:

Front rank:
> Spouses
> Parents

Second rank:
> Adult children
> Siblings

Third rank:
> Other relatives
> Friends and neighbours

The people who cared for members of the main sample of 'ordinary' attendance allowance claimants followed a similar pattern (Table 2).

Table 2   Kin-carers

Living in the same household
- 12   husbands or wives
- 5   mothers
- 5   daughters
- 1   brother

Living nearby
- 3   daughters/daughters-in-law
- 1   sister

No kin carer
- 2   formal arrangements

---

15 of the 29 disabled adults were married. All but three of the *husbands and wives* had adopted the role of chief carer, even though some elderly carers were hardly in the best of health themselves. The three exceptions were elderly partners who were incapable of providing care – indeed, they needed looking after almost as much as the members of our sample did. If you asked spouse-carers how they had adopted their role, they tended to describe how their husband or wife had fallen ill; caring was so automatic that it required no explanation. Husbands and wives nevertheless felt they owed a duty to their partners, which, for the most part, they accepted willingly:

> *She is my responsibility ... She was a woman who loved her kids*
> *... she was cooking good food. It was wonderful ... I will look*
> *after her right to the grave.*

Even so, the burden could be considerable, especially if the carer
had children or other sick or disabled relatives to look after as well.

> One woman had given up her part-time job to look after two
> severely disabled relatives. Her husband had suffered kidney
> failure and required regular dialysis. Her mother was a stroke
> victim paralysed, incontinent, partially blind and deaf, and
> confused.

Five unmarried young adults had been mentally handicapped since
birth. They had been looked after by their *mothers* throughout their
childhood, and this relationship continued after they had grown up.

So more than half of the people with disabilities were able to turn
to a 'front rank' relative – a partner or parent who accepted the
responsibility almost automatically.

For the remaining twelve disabled people there was no member of
the front rank available. These include the three couples in which both
husband and wife needed to be looked after. The interview
concentrated on what did happen, without looking in detail into what
alternatives might have been possible, so we do not have a full
description of the family trees of each of these people.

Five people were cared for by a *daughter* who lived with them,
and one by a *brother* living in the same house. Where the carer had
been living with the disabled person before he or she needed much
care, the change in relationships seemed to have happened without any
conscious decision on either side.

> An unmarried daughter had, for example, lived with her mother
> all her life, and had been laying plans for them both to retire to
> the seaside when she herself reached 60. For her, caring was
> as 'automatic' as if she had been a wife or mother.

> When her mother was first taken into hospital, the daughter had
> been asked whether she would like assistance with her mother's
> care, such as a home help for example. But she had replied
> simply "I prefer to do these things myself".

The outcome was less predictable when the disabled person was
not living with a relative at the time the need arose. In these cases
there were two or three people in the family who might have provided

care. Sometimes either the carer or the disabled person moved home so that they could live together.

Four other disabled people had carers from the second rank (a daughter, two daughters-in-law and a sister) who did not live with them, but who visited frequently. It was clear that people with disabilities could not live without a resident carer unless they were able to look after themselves at night and do at least some household tasks. Several of the non-resident carers were also able to share the work or the worry with other members of the family who lived locally. The non-resident solution would only work, therefore, in certain circumstances.

The final two people with disabilities had no kin carer and had to rely on more formal arrangements.

Shared or delegated care arrangements

Most of the disabled people in the main sample had one person who had accepted the responsibility for caring, and who did most of it personally. In these cases, the label 'carer' could be applied without any ambiguity. There were seven cases where the basic arrangements did not fit into so simple a pattern. Four of these cases involved payment for care.

Part-time carers

Two people with disabilities were able to look after themselves in their own homes, but relied on a relative to come in at fixed times to undertake tasks which they could not manage on their own. By implication, the helpers had only a slight responsibility outside their hours 'on duty', though each was no doubt available 'on call'.

> Mr Ericson was confined to a wheelchair, but was able to look after himself a lot of the time. He lived alone, and his sister came to help him three set times each week: an hour on Sunday, three hours each on Tuesday and Thursday. She brought shopping which she had already purchased, and helped with the housework. Mr Ericson had recently lost his attendance allowance, on the grounds that he no longer required constant care.

> Mrs Paxton was elderly and suffered from severe arthritis. She lived alone in a large private house, which she was finding increasingly difficult to manage. She said that she would soon have to give up the house and find a place in a sheltered home.

Her daughter-in-law lived nearby, and came in five and a half hours a day to provide care and domestic assistance.

Mrs Paxton paid most of her attendance allowance to her daughter-in-law who came in daily to look after her. As she said:

> *I've got to pay my daughter-in-law ... I can't expect her to do something for nothing.*

Shared care

Three disabled people had more than one carer.

Mrs Cox had difficulty in using her arms and legs: she had problems preparing food and drink for herself, and relied on a wheelchair for getting about out of doors. She lived with her husband and a lodger who has been a friend for 20 years. Mr Cox had full-time employment, but worked double shifts three days a week so that he had four days off. He cared for Mrs Cox when he was at home, and made sure that he did the intimate tasks before and after he went to work. But the friend, who was retired, looked after her when Mr Cox was at work. "He's better than an outsider", she said. He was, therefore, the 'carer' in the practical sense for much of the time, although the responsibility ultimately fell on Mr Cox.

Mrs Cox paid her attendance allowance direct to the friend and lodger who looked after her when her husband was out.

Mrs Demetriou had been hospitalised following a stroke, and had then stayed temporarily with her son and daughter-in-law. She was able to return home with her husband, but he was very frail and confused. Between them they could live on their own, but only with plenty of support. We interviewed the daughter-in-law who seemed to have taken on most of the responsibility for the old couple, but she described a joint caring arrangement which she thought was typical of a 'Mediterranean family'. The Demetrious had four sons who lived locally, and they and their wives all visited their parents almost daily. So did Mr Demetriou's sister. They made sure that the couple were all right, brought the shopping (often paid for out of their own pockets), cooked meals and did the laundry. They were in constant touch with each other by telephone if they did not meet at the couple's flat. There was, therefore, a large number of members of the family actively engaged in caring, though it was difficult to tell how evenly the load was shared.

Mrs Ellis had serious difficulties in moving about following operations on her legs. Her husband was also seriously disabled, and required more personal care than she did herself. They both lived with their daughter and her young family. But because the daughter was fully occupied with the father and her own baby, another daughter, living nearby, came in daily to look after their mother, and also to do the daily housework. The live-out daughter was regarded as the mother's carer, but clearly the two daughters formed a team.

Care packages

The two disabled people without any relative to take on the responsibility for their care had both made arrangements with more formal sources.

Mrs Wright and her husband were both wheelchair-bound. They had moved into a specially-adapted flat belonging to a housing association, which also ran a residential care home next door. Mrs Wright needed a minimum of 30 hours of care a week, to get her up in the morning, put her to bed and help her to the toilet. The care was provided by the staff of the residential home. She welcomed the chance to live in her own specially-adapted flat after years of being 'wrapped in cotton wool' in Part 3 accommodation. "Here it is more like home."

Mrs Wright paid her attendance allowance to the voluntary organisation which ran the nearby residential home whose staff provided care.

Ms Darley was the only person who had managed to piece together a complete care package for herself using local authority services. She had severe physical disabilities and spent most of her day in a wheelchair. She had limited use of one arm, with which she was able to feed herself. She lived alone in a specially- adapted flat in a sheltered housing scheme operated by the local authority. A care attendant employed by the social services came to her for three and a half hours each day. A community nurse visited at weekends, when the care assistant did not come. She also had a home help one and a half hours a week.

Ms Darley contributed £10 per week towards the cost of her social services. This was the minimum fee, determined by the fact that she was on income support.

Payment for primary care

None of the one-for-one carers who had taken on the full responsibility for the care of their disabled relatives were directly paid for their services, whether out of the attendance allowance or not. In practice, most of them had direct access to the attendance allowance money because they ran the household budget, but in no case was there any suggestion that it represented payment.

Nor, in the four cases involving payment, was there any suggestion of a strictly economic transaction, still less that the amount paid represented a fair evaluation of the work done.

- In the two cases where the payment was made to a friend or relative (Mrs Paxton's daughter-in-law and Mrs Cox's lodger) there is a strong presumption that the service might have been provided anyway. The transfer of the attendance allowance was a voluntary gesture of reciprocation on the part of the disabled person. It is nevertheless clear that the opportunity to offer payment made both Mrs Paxton and Mrs Cox feel happier about their relationship with their helpers, neither of whom was within the degrees of kinship bound by a caring obligation.

- In the two cases where the payment was made to an agency whose paid staff provided care (Mrs Wright's voluntary organisation, Ms Darley's social services department) both organisations were motivated by a commitment to service rather than by commercial considerations. The amount of the payment was, again, a token determined by their ability to pay, while the agency bore most of the financial costs of the arrangement from its central funds.

Help from organisations

All of the disabled people had received assistance or support at some time or other from the local authority social services department, and the local health authority. The most common forms of service, each mentioned by between a third and two-thirds of the sample, were:

- Advice about services from a *social worker*;
- *Physical aids*, such as wheelchairs, households gadgets and so on;
- Assistance with *transport*, including bus passes, taxi services;
- *Holidays* organised and/or subsidised by the council;
- *Home deliveries* of meals on wheels or incontinence pads.

Each of these services was valuable. Some of them, especially the home deliveries, effectively reduced the amount of work which had to be undertaken within the home. But they did not contribute directly to the claimant's regular need for care.

Mrs Wright and Ms Darley were receiving substantial domiciliary services from the local authority and a voluntary organisation respectively, because they had no informal carer. Only two other members of the sample were receiving any support services in the form of a helper who came into their home.

> Mrs Joseph's main carer was her husband. He remained in full-time work and was exceptionally busy trying to fulfil both roles. The social services department provided a home-help two hours per week, and a care assistant came one afternoon per fortnight.

> One other respondent was visited by a community nurse three mornings and seven evenings every week.

So only four people had domiciliary care in the sense of regular visits of personnel who helped care for the disabled person, or shared the housework. The OPCS disability survey showed that home helps were easily the most commonly available home service, provided to about a quarter of the most severely disabled people (severity grades 9 and 10) living in the community. Home-help provision varied according to the domestic situation of the person with a disability:

Single and living alone	75%
Married	25%
Single and living with others	10%

If these figures applied to our own small sample, we would have expected six or seven respondents to have been in receipt of domiciliary services; four is therefore on the low side. Either way, it is clear that the great majority of disabled people with kin carers had no support of this kind. The carers were left to do the work on their own. For some of them, of course, the job could be managed by one person without too much difficulty, and no help was needed. But for others, the burden of care was heavy, and some relief might have made all the difference.

Support services can also be provided outside the home, and this allows a measure of relief to carers. Five members of the sample were affected:

- Four of the five young adults with mental handicaps were attending training centres; one of them also stayed one night a week in a hostel, primarily to prepare her for the possibility of living apart from her parents when they could no longer look after her. Her mother paid £10 per week to the hostel.
- One woman went to hospital for two days and nights each week, to give her husband respite from his caring duties.

The remaining 20 people with disabilities did not have any regular caring services from official organisations, although they did have access to the other forms of support outlined at the beginning of this section.

Views about helping services

Some carers felt that caring for their relative was their own responsibility, or that the disabled person preferred kin to strangers.

> *I was a funny man myself. I didn't want nobody to help ... She's not easy to get on with. I felt I wanted to do it myself. (Husband of woman with mental illness.)*

A relatively small amount of help from the formal services could be exactly what was wanted:

> *She is my responsibility ... I don't phone them and ask them anything ... But a little bit of help here and there, it's just wonderful. Thank the Lord for it. (Husband who cared for wife who is a stroke victim.)*

However, others were critical of the level of support provided by the formal services. Several relatives remarked that while they were available and physically able to act as carers it seemed impossible to persuade the formal services to take on more responsibility.

> *My GP actually said to me when I was at breaking point ... "Go away and leave your mother"... But I couldn't do that ... leave her unattended in the house ... She's a human being ...I couldn't have driven off ... (Daughter of woman suffering from dementia.)*

Some felt that the formal services had almost conspired to force them to take on the full burden of responsibility for their disabled relative:

> *(When my husband came out of hospital) they said I could have all the help and support that was possible. But I didn't have*

anything other than a nurse come in every Wednesday to give him a blanket bath. (Wife of man suffering the effects of a stroke.)

They all tell me I look after her so well that I don't really need help. (Daughter of woman who has suffered severe strokes.)

Some people complained that the range of duties home helps were allowed or were willing to do was too narrow for their purposes. One disabled person complained that home helps would not 'cross the barrier' to do 'nursing' tasks, such as emptying commodes or giving a person a bath. Another felt that they were unreliable:

They don't turn up or they change ... I've been about five weeks without anybody ... They are not particularly over-enthusiastic, some of them, to help ... Some of them are just plain lazy. (Woman confined to a wheelchair.)

Mr Andrews said his greatest difficulties were first thing in the morning, and when school closed at 3.30pm – which was when his children needed looking after as well as his wife. Finding it impossible to cope alone, he investigated ways of bringing in another helper to share the care. He discovered that the health authority nurses were fully stretched, and unable to help his wife. He considered private nurses, but had to abandon the idea on the grounds of cost. Then he approached the local social services to see if it would be possible to get a home help from 8 to 10am and from 3.30 to 6pm each day. But he was told that, because he was in employment, his case did not have high priority, and therefore he would only be able to get a home help between 10am and 3.30pm – precisely the time when he did not need one!

Mr Andrews observed that the level of support provided had always seemed to be the minimum necessary to sustain him in his role as carer. For example, it was only when he himself became ill that his wife was offered two nights a week of care in hospital, to give him a break: 'If you don't do this', his GP said, 'you are ... going to crack up completely, and that wouldn't do either of you any benefit'. On another occasion, when he slipped a disc lifting his wife into the bath, he said that the hospital ...

> *... gave me top priority for hydrotherapy and all the rest of it to get me fit. With a smile, if you like, they said "the quicker we get you fit, the quicker you can look after your wife again".*

On the other hand, others had a higher opinion of these services:

The home help is marvellous, and most of them are. (Carer of woman with dementia.)

One of the features of the new arrangements for community care following the Griffiths Report will be 'care managers' – people who would assess the client's needs, and put together a package of services and benefits, and act as a source of advice and back-up. Several people recognised the need for a single point of contact with public services; and wanted to feel that someone was keeping an eye on their needs.

Nobody comes to see if you're cracking up ... There aren't enough social workers ... If you feel suicidal, no-one would know. (Daughter of woman suffering from dementia.)

One partially paralysed woman felt that she had been able to take the care manager role herself; but she recognised that not every one could be expected to:

I had lots of people in the beginning – lots ... I (sorted it out) with the central care people ... I'm lucky, I can do that. Some people can't ... I know what to do.

But others had not been successful in their attempts to obtain help from official organisations. They felt that they should not have to ask – they should be told:

I think that a social worker should come and assess the whole situation and tell you what is available for you. You shouldn't be asking, because half the time you don't know. (Daughter-in-law, working part-time, of elderly disabled woman.)

For those who did ask for help, securing support was often a laborious and frustrating experience.

You can apply and apply (to social services) and in the end you are talking about waiting for six months to get something done. So you end up doing it yourself. (Daughter-in-law of stroke victim.)

One carer was so upset by the way she felt she was treated by officialdom that she assumed that our request to talk about her mother's attendance allowance would be some sort of check that she was not 'pocketing the money':

*You've got no back-up of any sort. You feel like you are on your
own ... and you are clawing for everything that you can get. And
you don't even know what you are allowed to get anyway ... You
feel like you're being treated like some sort of gold-scrounging
criminal ... The incontinence service called and said 'Why are
you using so many?' and I was just thinking, well this is terrible
... that you should be accused of stealing incontinence pads!*

Help from informal sources

We have already described the arrangement whereby the role of 'key
carer' had been shared more or less equally between an elderly
couple's four sons, four daughters-in-law and a sister. In that case,
clearly, there was plenty of mutual support within the family. Another
family, already described, had arranged for one daughter to care for
the mother, and another for the father; again, this was an arrangement
where mutual support was built in.

Other carers received regular, perhaps daily, assistance with caring
from relatives living in their home or in the area. Several elderly
couples, the one caring for the other, had help with their daily chores
from a daughter who lived nearby. Where a live-in carer had a family
of her own, her teenage sons or daughters might provide a 'sitting'
service for the disabled member of the household when she went out.
It was normal, however, for intimate care to be the responsibility of
the main carer alone.

Other carers said that they had some irregular but valuable
assistance from the wider family. For example, a relative might take
care of the disabled person at weekends from time to time.

> The brother of a woman caring for their arthritic mother came
> each year from Cornwall to take the mother back to his family,
> to give the main carer a break.

But other carers had much less help from the family. In these cases,
the only involvement seemed to be paying social visits and perhaps
contributing gifts. Relatives who lived away from the disabled
person's home and had homes and families of their own to look after
did not appear to be expected to contribute significantly to the task of
caring.

Even members of the family living locally could not necessarily
be relied on to help more than occasionally.

> Mrs Eldridge had arthritis and lived with her husband. Their
> daughter came in regularly to help with housework. But their

son, who also lived locally, had always been fairly distant from his parents. He visited only occasionally, and provided little help.

Help was not always available even from people living in the same house. While some carers described the contributions provided by their husbands or teenage children, others commented wrily that their own sons and daughters did little to help beyond preparing drinks, or occasionally sitting in in the evenings. One carer remarked about her children that, 'you can't put upon them too often.'

Friends were less likely than relatives to provide significant assistance to the key carer. However, there were some notable exceptions to this generalisation:

> The friend who lodged with Mr and Mrs Cox regularly looked after her when her husband was at work. In fact the family described him as her 'carer', though the husband seemed to us to have retained the principal role.

> An elderly couple had a friend who came in two hours a week to help the caring husband with the housework – 'she keeps us all nice and clean and tidy'.

> A frail elderly woman relied on a younger friend for the kind of domestic assistance that some other disabled people received from home helps.

> Another friend regularly 'sat in' one afternoon a week, so that the disabled woman's husband could have a break.

> Mr and Mrs Wright, whose basic care needs were provided by the workers from a nearby old person's home, had friends from their local church who provided the additional essential assistance that allowed them to remain in the community. These friends accompanied Mrs Wright on her regular hospital visits and on shopping trips, when she needed assistance with her wheelchair.

A few other disabled people said that they received assistance with their care needs from friends, though on an occasional rather than a regular basis. In some instances, the disabled person said that they liked to give a small payment or gift to their friends when they helped in this way: they felt awkward about 'imposing' on their friends too much, or exploiting their goodwill.

Payment for help

We have seen that a few people with disabilities paid their principal carer, usually a sum which bore no direct relation to the extent of the work the carers did. A few attendance allowance claimants paid for smaller amounts of help.

> Mrs Bull paid her daughter £25 per week to help her caring husband with the domestic work – shopping, cleaning, ironing and so on.

> Mr and Mrs Miston paid their friend who helped with the housework, but there was 'no set amount'; they seemed to give her what they could each week, sometimes 'in kind'.

This latter case was the nearest we found to a paid neighbour, but it was clearly an informal arrangement.

Two people paid for regular treatment to help alleviate their physical disability: one woman had weekly instruction from a yoga teacher and a man paid for weekly visits from a physiotherapist.

Some people hired help on an occasional basis. A husband who worked full time recently paid a cleaner to do two days spring-cleaning, and said that he would like to buy in more domestic assistance or care in this way, but could not afford it. Other bought-in services included gardening, household repairs and decorating.

In spite of the scarcity of paid support, disabled people and their carers could identify some potential advantages. Payment could make the arrangement acceptable to the disabled person and carer alike – 'you can't take advantage', as one disabled person put it. Disabled people who relied on friends to do 'odd jobs' around the house, or to accompany them when they went shopping, similarly felt more comfortable if they could give their friend a small payment or 'treat'.

Few people with disabilities could rely on regular, unpaid assistance from friends and relatives other than their key carer. Payment might have enabled the disabled person to ask for help without feeling so dependent on people's sense of duty or generosity because they are giving something in return. One disabled person felt that, without paying the helper, 'the commitment will fizzle out'.

Some people with disabilities recognised that paying for care could give them more control over the kind of services that were provided to them. One disabled couple who were unhappy about the service they received from home helps said that they wished they could pay directly for domestic help:

> *You have to just accept whoever comes ... Because they are not paid by you, they are only ... answerable to their governors – who never come and see the work they do. So there's no control ... A few weeks ago I asked the lady to wipe the window sill. – 'I am not supposed to wipe paint work.' – I couldn't believe it ... it's ridiculous really.*

References

1. Reviewed by G. Parker, *With Due Care and Attention*, Family Policy Studies Centre, 1990.
2. H. Qureshi and A. Walker, *The Caring Relationship*, Macmillan, 1989.

2 Sources of income

Claimants' and partners' incomes

Some social security benefits, including the attendance allowance, are paid to individuals without regard to their family circumstances. Entitlement to other benefits, including the retirement pension and invalidity benefit, is based on the individual, but the amount paid can be influenced by his or her commitments to support a spouse and/or children. A third group of benefits, including income support, assumes that husbands, wives and children share their income and expenditure, and entitlement is based on the family unit. Because of the importance of income support in setting a baseline income against which other resources should be compared, this section considers the combined incomes available to disabled people and their partners.

The growth in the number of two-earner families makes this view of married couples as a single income unit increasingly out of date in many social groups. But the married couples in this sample were not two-earner families, and retained the traditional assumption that the income of either was available to be spent on the needs of both. They operated a common purse, usually handled by the caring partner.

Some members of the sample had close kin who lived with them, or in the vicinity, who might add to the resources available to the disabled person. The British social security system treats the incomes of adults who are not married to each other as almost entirely independent of each other. The incomes of caring kin, and the financial relationships between carers and people with disabilities will therefore be treated in a separate section.

The analysis of disabled people's income needs to be set in the context of the baseline provided by income support. The scheme offers a minimum income to people not in full-time work which can be augmented by premiums based on age and disability. (Children are left out of this description; only a few claimants in the sample had any.) The weekly income (excluding rent and rates rebates) guaranteed to a single person with the attendance allowance (at 1988 rates) was:

	Single person	Couple
Income support basic	£33.40	£51.45
Severe disability premium	£24.75	£24.75
Attendance allowance (higher)	<u>£32.95</u>	<u>£32.95</u>
Total	£91.10	£109.15

(Mobility allowance, if paid, would be in addition to this.) These amounts compare with the basic level of income support (for single people without disabilities) of only £33.40 (single) or £51.45 (married). The extras reflect an official view that the minimum needs of seriously disabled people are considerably higher than those of people who are unable to work for reasons other than disability. The income base for people relying purely on social security benefits is therefore higher for attendance allowance claimants than for the rest of the population, but only part of this extra consists of the allowance itself.

A corollary is that someone entitled to attendance allowance would be highly likely to qualify for income support and housing benefit. Pensioners, for example, would need independent means of at least £15 per week to add to their basic state pensions in order to lift themselves clear of income support; more to be clear of housing benefit.

For these reasons, incomes of attendance allowance claimants can be simplified into three categories: those who relied (almost) entirely on state benefits and would therefore have qualified for income support; those with fairly substantial pensions from former employers, or with other resources of their own; and those with an income from employment. This small sample is not suitable for describing the levels of income available to disabled people in detail. The OPCS disability survey provides information which is fuller and more accurate.[1] We will simply compare the experience of claimants in each of the three categories.

Among this sample of 29, none of the people with disabilities was in employment. Only one member of the sample had worked in the recent past; none of the others considered going out to work as an option.

However a working husband or wife could have made all the difference to their level of income. In fact, only three partners worked – all husbands, all of them full time. Two had sole care of their wives. They were kept exceptionally busy as they struggled to fit their caring and domestic duties into their working day. Their lives were among the most exhausting and physically stressful of any of the carers.

> On the day Mr Joseph was interviewed, he had been up at 7am to get his wife out of bed and his teenage son off to school. He was due to start his eight hour shift at work at noon. His school-age son would help look after his mother when he returned from school at 4pm, and an older son would look in when he finished work in the early evening. All the time Mr Joseph was being interviewed, he was busy washing pots, tidying and making his wife drinks.

> Mr Joseph regretted that he was unable to work overtime or at weekends, because the family needed the money to pay the mortgage on their terraced house. He suffered from a stomach disorder which he put down to having to eat too fast and at irregular intervals. However, he was reconciled to his lot, and felt that he owed it to his wife to care for her.

One full-time worker had arranged to share his caring duties with an old friend who lived with him and his wife – Mr and Mrs Cox, described in Chapter 1. He had had to alter his hours of work to allow time to undertake his share of the caring, but the arrangement appeared to be working reasonably well.

In principle, one option might be for people to continue working and use their earnings to pay for someone else to care for their disabled relative. The arrangement between the Coxes and their friend has some similarities with such a plan, but no-one in the main sample of attendance allowance claimants had a straightforward substitute carer paid for out of earnings.

None of the worker/carer husbands was able to draw a high wage. But at least they were better off than those reliant on ordinary state benefits.

Some husbands or wives were unable to work in their own right; they had retired or had a disability themselves. Others had given up work in order to care for the disabled claimant. So very few families (3 out of 29) combined the attendance allowance with earnings. All the others were more or less dependent on other social security benefits.

Among claimants without earnings, some of them were confused, and it was not easy to sort out what they were getting from which sources. But some of them were retired people or widows who had an occupational pension or other resources which, when added to their state pension or invalidity benefit, lifted their income clear of the basic benefit zone.

> Mrs Ling had a war widow's pension of £63 per week, plus an occupational pension of her own of about £50. She reckoned that interest on her savings added about £20 per week to her regular income.

But the majority of people with disabilities had little or no income derived from previous employment. These included some who had retired without an adequate occupational pension, as well as those who had become disabled before they could build up pension rights. The latter group included, of course, the five young people who had been handicapped from birth, who relied on income support for their basic benefit.

The combination of an income guarantee rather higher than is paid to unemployed people and lack of independent resources means that the incomes of attendance allowance claimants filled rather a narrow range, with few very low, and none very high. The same narrow band is revealed by the much larger sample studied by OPCS: compared with the national distribution of net incomes, many severely disabled people were in the middle of the range; few were found at the top or the bottom of the range.[1]

Indeed the categorisation between those with earnings, those with occupational pensions and those with neither meant a lot in terms of the composition of people's incomes, but did not make all that much difference to the total amount. The crucial point for claimants was receipt of the attendance allowance and/or the mobility allowance. Up to £80 per week could hang on that pair of assessments.

Incomes and contributions of relatives

It was shown in Chapter 1 that, apart from the 12 people with disabilities who were cared for by their husband or wife, a further 11 were cared for by a close relative who lived in the same house, but who formed a separate 'income unit' as defined for social security purposes. Most of them were women – the mother or the daughter of the attendance allowance claimant.

In principle relatives might be able to combine work and caring in a marital partnership: one person caring, the other working full-time to provide an income for the whole household. In practice though, only three of the eleven live-in kin carers were married. The husbands of two of them were in full-time work with good earnings. The other was as disabled as the member of our sample, so the daughter cared for two people without any earned income.

Some non-married carers worked part-time, having adapted their working hours to suit their double responsibilities. Another source of income was an occupational pension drawn by a carer in her own right.

So several live-in carers had some income from employment, either directly or indirectly. But others had to rely entirely on social security benefits.

The question about whether live-in carers contributed to the financial support of people with disabilities was rather academic in most cases: those on social security, and many of those with part-time earnings, were no better off than the disabled person they cared for. Their financial contribution took the form of the loss of their own earning power, rather than adding to the resources available to be spent on goods or services.

Most of the live-in carers operated joint household budgets. The mothers who had been looking after mentally handicapped children from birth simply carried on with the housekeeping as they always had done, and the one handicapped child with a working father benefited from his earnings in much the same unquestioned way as she would have done when she was younger. Some of these mothers were conscious of spending the child's income, including the attendance allowance, on items specifically for the child; but they had no concept of their own income, *not* to be spent on the child. All of these young people had a mental handicap, and their mothers took most decisions on their behalf; perhaps a different relationship would have developed if the handicap had been physical.

The daughters who lived with their disabled parent all ran joint household budgets. If the parent's disability was purely physical, the supervision of the housekeeping money tended to be shared between them; if the dependant suffered from dementia, the carer tended to take complete charge. A distinction might be made between 'my' money and 'your' money, but a good deal of it was pooled, and there was no sign that either member of the household preserved income in order to maintain a higher standard of living than the other. Few of them had the resources for a high standard of living anyway; but where they did, it was shared.

As far as live-in kin carers are concerned then, income and resources tended to be pooled, but this involved few transfers between income units because the carer's income was usually almost as low as the disabled person's. Nevertheless, most live-in carers would have seen it as their responsibility to purchase something that the disabled person needed, without considering whose money it was.

When kin carers lived separately from the people they looked after, household budgets were much more likely to be kept separate from each other. In this category we identified:

> A daughter who had given up work to look after her mother, while her sister looked after their father; although the sister's husband had a job, both families felt very poor, as described below;

> A team of sons and daughters-in-law, apparently led by one of the latter, all of whom had jobs. The carers were spending a lot of their own money on things for the old couple, without any regular arrangement for doing so.

> A daughter-in-law with a working husband. Since she was paid for her services, it is unlikely that much income flowed in the other direction.

> A sister who came in to help her brother, who was confined to a wheelchair, at set times each week. This man was among the least dependent members of the sample, and, again, the two households kept their money separately.

So only one of the live-out kin carers seemed to be using some of their income to contribute to the welfare of their disabled relative.

Apart from their immediate carers, several people with disabilities had other relatives, often a son or daughter, who might have contributed to their income. In this sample, there were no kin who had made a regular arrangement to pay so much per week or per month to top up their social security benefits. But several kin were 'very good to me' with occasional support – paying electricity or phone bills, bringing food or other gifts when they visited and so on.

> *Our daughter works for a butcher: she brings in meat every*
> *week ... My brother bought us the video ... we wouldn't have*
> *that otherwise ... If I said 'now I'm short of continental quilts'*
> *... the children would help out.*

But other relatives, close both in kinship and in travelling distance,
appeared to make no contribution of this sort.

> *Do our children give us money? ... Our children would take*
> *money from us if they could!*

It cannot be said that a clear picture of relatives' financial
contribution to disabled people's welfare has emerged. We are just
starting a larger scale study which is designed to examine the question
in more detail. But, in summary:

- no relatives had assigned a fixed slice of their income to
  support a member of this sample; this is in contrast to the
  Bexley sample, where regular payments from kin were an
  important source of money.
- most relatives who lived with the person they cared for had
  blurred the distinction between their own money and the
  disabled person's.
- this could lead to implicit transfers; but most of the kin who
  had accepted the main responsibility were little better off than
  the disabled person they cared for.

Feelings about benefits

The people with disabilities in this sample, and many of the relatives
who cared for them, were unable to go out to work to earn a living; so
they did not feel that they had any choice but to rely on benefits as
their main source of income. Some of them, especially those who had
been disabled for many years, or who had relied on their pensions long
before their disability affected them, were so used to the idea of relying
on social security that they did not comment directly. But others were
unhappy about the experience.

Some people said that it hurt their pride to have to live on benefits.

> One woman, who had first applied for attendance allowance and
> been refused when her mentally handicapped daughter was a
> baby, had been dissuaded from applying again by her husband:
>
> > *My husband was that type of man. He said 'well it's*
> > *charity, forget it'.*

As a result she had only applied again for attendance allowance (successfully on this occasion) six years ago, and consequently missed out on up to 12 years of potential attendance allowance payments.

Some carers and disabled people said that they spent hours on the telephone or queuing at their local social security office if they needed advice, or had a problem; and then often, as one carer put it 'everyone passes the buck to a different department'.

One woman recalled how she and her husband had had 'a terrible job' getting on to social security when they lost their job managing a shop as a result of her disability: 'We waited months. We went through nearly all our savings.'

Others were just confused:

Benefits is a jungle ... people understand their bit of it, but there's no way of overall understanding it.

Some disabled people wanted benefits advice from someone outside the DSS. On the other hand, some of the social workers we interviewed felt that they did not know enough about the complex system of benefits available to disabled people to give good advice. They might pass on enquiries to specialist welfare rights workers. But this meant that a disabled person had to go to one person to find out about care and another to find out about their financial position, even though the two were closely inter-related.

Some claimants felt bitter when they compared their lot with that of other people on benefits:

I'm not mentioning no names, but it really annoys me when they can say they go out this day and that day – 'Oh, I bought a dress for myself. I bought a pair of shoes for myself.' I can't keep on doing that. (Mother of mentally handicapped girl.)

Because of all these problems with claiming and living on benefits some people simply chose to close off their mind to the possibility that there might be other benefits which they could claim:

Right now I think there is even a little more one could get. But ... I just get on with what I have and don't worry about these things. (Man caring for his wife who is a stroke victim.)

For people with little cash to spare who depended on benefits, every review of their allowances, or every change in government policy could be frightening.

When the benefits system changed in April 1988, one disabled woman was panicked into thinking that she would lose half her benefits, and phoned up her social security office 'in a terrible state'.

Another disabled woman who was receiving income support said that she secretly maintained a small savings account in order to protect her against the insecurity of living on benefits. She argued that if she didn't do this, then if her benefits were ever cut, she might be unable to pay her telephone bill, for example. She did not want to risk having her telephone cut off – she depended on it too heavily.

Claiming attendance allowance

There was no single method by which the disabled people in our sample had found out about the attendance allowance. In most cases, there had been a delay between the onset of a person's illness or disability and their application for the allowance; and in some cases the interval stretched to many years.

Many people who had spent time in hospital had been informed about the attendance allowance (and perhaps other benefits) by the hospital welfare officers or by other medical staff. Sometimes it was the nurse who visited the disabled person at home when they were discharged from hospital who had told them about the allowance.

Households who lived mainly on state benefits tended to have intermittent contacts with welfare rights officers, social workers, or citizen's advice bureaux; and information about attendance allowance had often been passed on through these sources. Mothers of mentally handicapped children tended to rely on the schools and day centres their children went to, and the network of other mothers of mentally handicapped children, for their initial information about attendance allowance and their advice about benefits generally. Other people had learned about attendance allowance through friends or other relatives, by picking up a form at the Post Office, or from a television programme.

Most claimants had applied for the attendance allowance as soon as they found out that it existed. However, some people had been more reticent, either because they were not sure whether they qualified or because they were generally reluctant to claim benefits.

Mrs Staines received industrial injuries benefit in addition to her old age pension and her daughter had a pension from her former employer. The daughter felt that they could manage fairly comfortably on their income, but felt sorry for disabled people who had only the minimum level of state benefits to survive on: 'they must be in dire straits sometimes'.

Mrs Staines's daughter was persuaded to apply for attendance allowance for her mother by the local geriatric welfare officer. The first time he gave her the form and told her that she should apply, Miss Staines felt unhappy about claiming benefits, and had put the form away in a drawer. When the welfare officer visited again, some time later, he was firm.

> *At the time there was quite a furore raging in the local press which had publicised a story about a disabled person getting two agency nurses to look after her, which was costing the council £800 a week. 'You've seen that piece in the paper', the welfare officer said, 'you're saving the council £800 a week looking after your mother the way you do. You apply for it!'*

There was also pressure on Mrs Staines' daughter from other people she knew:

> *(They) said 'you really should apply'. I wouldn't have bothered with it in the first place but for them all ganging up on me!*

On the other hand, a few people had had what one carer called 'a fight on my hands' to get the attendance allowance, having to apply more than once before getting the allowance. Some people objected to the way the medical examination had been carried out by the doctor who came to assess them.

> One disabled woman, who had applied four times before she had got the allowance, said that she had got 'fed up' with doctors coming and hitting her feet and knees with hammers.

> The daughter of one frail old woman had been reluctant to apply for the attendance allowance at first, simply because she knew that her mother found medical examinations a strain.

Two disabled people in our sample had just had their attendance allowance cancelled following a medical review, or had been informed that it soon would be cancelled. They could not understand the inconsistency between the assessments made by the different doctors who had come to see them, since neither of them felt that their health had improved.

Reference

1. J. Martin and A. White, *The Financial Circumstances of Disabled People Living in Private Households*, HMSO, 1988.

3 Patterns of expenditure

What people thought the attendance allowance was for
It has never been clearly stated what the attendance allowance is for. It is awarded on the basis of a medical assessment of the extent to which claimants need frequent attention in connection with their bodily functions, *or* require supervision to avoid substantial danger to themselves or others.

- Both the name, and the basis for assessment, might imply that the benefit is intended in one way or another to help meet the costs of the care which is the defining criterion. This would make the 'attendance' allowance directly analogous to the 'mobility' allowance: the latter is unambiguously aimed at helping people who cannot walk, to pay for alternative means of transport.
- An alternative interpretation is that the attendance allowance is intended more generally to contribute to the whole range of additional costs associated with disability, including heating, laundry, food and so on. According to this hypothesis the attendance criterion is simply a way of identifying people whose disability is serious, and likely to cause such extra costs.

Whatever the general intention, there is no doubt at all that claimants are entitled to spend the money as they choose, without any suggestion that they 'ought' to be spending it on approved purposes.

But it is still relevant to ask what claimants thought the purpose of the benefit was, as well as what use they themselves put it to. Most disabled people or their carers did not have a fixed concept of the purpose of the benefit: they had not been told what to spend it on, so they had to guess. Many of them agreed with each suggestion that was made to them. Others threw the dilemma straight back at us by saying that it was for either purpose:

> *It's for people who need attendance ... For people to come in to get them washed and dressed ... And for the additional expenses.*

Four strands of thought could nevertheless be identified among people's responses to this question:

Paying for care: to pay for outside carers,
                   to support kin carers;
Extra expenses: to cover additional basic costs;
                   to allow for 'little extras'.

The first view was that the allowance was intended to be spent on cash payments to people – presumably non-relatives – who would come in to provide care. That was the clearest link between money and 'attendance'.

An example of that position was provided by the wheelchair-bound husband of a woman who was receiving attendance allowance: he said that he did not receive the allowance because he did not have an (outside) carer, whereas his wife did. He had, in fact, applied in the past, and been turned down. But other potential claimants may have failed to claim their entitlement because of a similar misunderstanding of the word 'attendance'. [Indeed, a personal acquaintance of one of the authors cared for her aged mother for ten years, but claimed the attendance allowance only in the final months when an agency nurse was hired to do night duty.]

On the other hand, several people commented that the amount of the benefit was far too small to pay for the level of attendance on which the assessment was based.

> *It's to make your life easier by being able to pay for extra help. But it doesn't work out like that, because to pay for help, where are you going to get anyone who will accept £30 a week? (Wheelchair-bound woman living alone.)*

The other view of the 'paying for care' version of the allowance's objectives was that it was aimed at the kin carers. Some saw this in general terms...

> *It's to pay me to attend to her – when she wants anything, to get it for her.*

Others made a direct comparison between the attendance allowance paid in support of a kin carer and the much higher costs of institutional care...

> *It's cheaper than being in hospital. That's the chief reason they give it, isn't it? (Husband of frail elderly woman.)*

> *It's to help you look after the disabled person. But they can't pay me to look after Jane. No way. Because it's a full-time job ... If she was in a home, it would cost £250 a week. (Mother of mentally handicapped girl.)*

But there were several forthright comments on the level of the benefit in comparison with the wages which a carer might have foregone. One respondent was outraged at the suggestion that attendance allowance could be seen in this way:

> *I think if you put it like that, that is a bloody cheek!*

Those who saw the allowance in terms of an addition to basic spending money also saw it in two ways.

- Some specifically mentioned the extra necessities like heating and laundry which had to be bought by, or on behalf of, the disabled person.
- Others saw the the money as going towards 'little extras' which might make life more tolerable in spite of the discomfort and inactivity suffered by people who could not take part in 'normal' activities. People commented that the attendance allowance 'sort of bucks up your income', provides a few 'comforts' or 'a bit of icing on the cake'.

For those members of our sample who were living on the margins of poverty, attendance allowance was a vital part of the family budget.

> One elderly disabled man said that, without the attendance allowance, 'It'd be murder ... we wouldn't be able to manage'. If his allowance was stopped, he said, then he would have to get rid of his television which he relied on 'to keep me occupied ... Otherwise I'd be looking at the four walls all day.'

The 'little extras' approach seemed to be associated with a better basic balance between income and needs. As one carer said, even without the allowance, her disabled mother 'would have still had (her extras). I'd have seen to that'. Another respondent illustrated the contrast more directly:

The widowed mother of a mentally handicapped girl said that the attendance allowance helped to pay for their car, without which she would have been unable to take her daughter to evening classes or to social events run by the local branch of Mencap. She was expecting to retire from her part-time job soon and added:

> *At the moment (the attendance allowance is) an added extra, but it will be essential when I don't go to work.*

Most of the carers drew the attendance allowance from the Post Office on behalf of the person they cared for. Some commented that it made no sense to pay the allowance to the disabled person, since they were often physically unable to collect it. Some of those who felt that the allowance should essentially be a payment for care, also wondered whether it should not be paid to the carer:

> *It should really be for my husband, shouldn't it? ... I suppose it's got to be made payable to me or else there could be a swizzle. (Disabled woman cared for by husband.)*

When asked about how they actually used the attendance allowance, or what difference it had made to their circumstances, a few were able to mention a direct link between the benefit and payments for care, as described later. But most disabled people and their carers said that they used the attendance allowance to supplement their household budget. Most households drew the attendance allowance weekly, or every few weeks, and used the money on shopping and everyday expenses. This was in contrast to the way some of them used other sources of income, such as mobility allowance (which was often allocated specifically to the costs of transport) or occupational pensions (which some people tried to save to meet large bills, or as a cushion for use in emergencies).

Some carers wanted to make the point that all the money was spent on the disabled person to whom the allowance was paid.

> The mother of a mentally handicapped young man said that she often left her son's allowance in the Post Office for a few weeks, then drew it out to buy him some new clothes that he needed.

> The mother of a mentally handicapped woman said that she paid part of the attendance allowance towards an insurance policy for her daughter so that 'if something happens to me, maybe someone will use it to look after her'.

One good way of discussing the impact of the attendance allowance was to ask how people would be affected if they did not have it. For two members of the sample, that was all too real a prospect – their allowance had been cancelled. They were actively contemplating the economies they would need to make.

> Mrs Halliday suffers from a painful condition affecting the nervous system which means that she can walk only for short distances, with the aid of a stick. She and her husband live in what they describe as a 'rough' council block, and have no car. Because Mrs Halliday cannot use public transport, she rarely goes out. She passes the time by knitting and reading magazines. They save up her mobility allowance and rent a car twice a year for a short holiday with a relative who lives by the sea. At Christmas they treat themselves by renting a video so that they can watch some films.

> Now that the attendance allowance is being stopped, Mrs Halliday said:

> > *It means that I won't be able to save all my mobility allowance. So that will cut down the outings in the summer ... (At the moment) I buy a bit of wool to knit and that to pass my time away – I shall have to stop that ... There won't be a video, not this year. Those little extras, they give you a few little pleasures. When you don't go out much you want something don't you?*

Standards of living

Most people with disabilities and their carers said that they had to manage their money carefully to make ends meet. In some households, money worries were so severe that the problems caused by disability almost seemed minor in comparison:

> Mr and Mrs Margolis were the couple in their fifties, both disabled, who were looked after by their two daughters working as a team. The household income consisted of Mr Margolis's invalidity benefit (£73), Mrs Margolis's higher rate attendance allowance and mobility allowance (total £56 a week) and the earnings of the son-in-law who lived with the couple (less than £100 a week). The daughter who lived nearby claimed income support.

> The daughters said that the family's main problem was the maintenance and upkeep of their terraced house, which was damp and in poor repair. There were two mortgages – the

second one having been taken out to try to tackle the damp. Mrs Margolis's condition tended to deteriorate in cold weather, yet the system of heating by electric fires was inefficient and expensive: the annual cost of gas and electricity was around £800.

The daughters said that they could not afford the warm clothing that Mrs Margolis needed – woollen tights, slippers, jumpers and warm dresses and nightdresses. They did not have a car, and so Mrs Margolis rarely went out. One daughter described their difficulties as follows:

> *The main thing is the money problem ... It weighs me down ... Sometimes I feel really low, you know. It breaks me down ... because I need to get (my mother) things and ... I need the money for myself.*

Mrs Margolis's case was not an isolated one. Other disabled people and their carers spoke about having rent arrears or fuel debts to pay. Asked whether they managed to save anything out of their weekly income, many people indicated that the very idea was unthinkable: 'you must be joking!'

> One cold afternoon, the interviewer called to talk to an elderly disabled woman, Mrs Patel, and the husband who cared for her. She found the couple in bed, trying to keep warm. It turned out to be Mr Patel's eightieth birthday! The interview was carried out by the warmth of a one-bar electric fire in the sitting room. Mr Patel said that their joint weekly income was only £69. Fortunately he had some savings which he was using to 'take advantage' of the Government's 'selling off everything' by buying shares which had quickly increased their value. The high point of Mr Patel's day was to spend part of the morning in the local library, reading the newspapers he could not afford to buy. He complained about the price of rice and said that 'Since I retired (12 years ago) I've not bought a single piece of clothing. I can't afford it.'

The people with disabilities and their carers were asked what kinds of things they could not afford, or what they would buy if they received a sudden windfall. In many cases the things they said they needed were all directly related to the physical needs of the disabled person: better heating, more clothes or bedding, an electric wheelchair to help them get about, a microwave to make it easier for a person in a wheelchair to cook for themselves. Many disabled people spent most of their time in their own home, and said that they would love a car so that they could get out more. A large number said that they had not had a holiday recently; others said that they used to go on council-subsidised holidays, but that these had been cut recently.

At the opposite end of the scale, of course, some people with disabilities lived in comfortable households with the financial means to overcome many of the practical problems caused by the disability.

> One retired couple had done everything possible to limit the restrictions the husband's stroke and confinement to a wheelchair had put on their lives. The garden had been turned into a patio, to reduce the amount of work, and Mr Goodwin paid a physiotherapist to help him with exercises on two mornings a week. The couple went out to the local park together every day and had two or three short holidays a year. In the past, their hobby had been amateur dramatics, and from time to time they took a taxi to the theatre eight miles away to see a play.

As the Goodwins' case indicates, those with adequate incomes spent a fair proportion of their money on things which they needed only because of their disability, or which cost extra because they could not do things 'normally'. Other costs incurred by people with adequate resources included adaptations to their home (building an extension or a downstairs toilet), and holidays (paying for an escort to accompany the disabled person, for example).

It has to be assumed that these better-off households' consumption of other goods and services was reduced, compared with what they would have been able to buy if they had no disability. If so they suffered a financial loss, even though they were not necessarily poor.

For the worse-off members of the sample, on the other hand, the need to spend extra on particular items because they were disabled might reduce their standard of living to a very low level. The OPCS survey attempted to measure the extra costs of disability[1]. It suggested that average additional expenditure averaged about £11 per week for people with very severe disabilities, though the figure rose to more than £15 per week for those who were better-off. The OPCS findings have been challenged by the Disablement Income Group, whose own enquiry suggested additional costs more like £70 per week.[2] For our own research, respondents were simply asked to describe their expenditure in general terms, so that we could compare that with other uses of their income.

The extent of these additional costs varied according to the particular circumstances. No one said they had none; several reported extra costs which were substantial, or would have been if the resources had been available to spend. Sometimes costs were 'out of control' because the person with the disability was not capable of limiting them.

> *The heating bill is astronomical – £180 a quarter. She doesn't understand how to get into bed to keep herself warm. She just wanders, crying, at night, so you've got to keep it heated ... Things go missing, including money ... One day she decided to cut the net curtains in half. (Daughter of woman suffering from dementia.)*

Another general effect of disability on household economies was the reluctance of carers to impose a cheese-paring regime on a loved-one who had such a bad time anyway. They might have been prepared to budget more strictly for themselves, but not for their disabled dependant.

The attendance allowance represented a substantial proportion of the income of people who lived largely on social security benefits. Of course, all the people in this sample were receiving the allowance, so we have no direct evidence about how they would have spent their money without it. But on the basis of the accounts we were given, one answer to the question about what the attendance allowance was used for is 'basic living expenses':

- For the poorest, it was having to be spent on the absolute basics that anyone else with a restricted income would be worrying about: food, fuel, clothes and so on.
- For people whose budget was better balanced, it was still going on basics, but could stretch to cover some of the extra basic costs imposed by disability: food, fuel, clothes and so on.
- People with a higher standard living were able to spend some money on items which made living with disability more tolerable. But it could still be argued that it was the allowance which allowed them to do that without eating into the income needed to pay for the same basics – food, fuel, clothes and so on – as everyone else was worried about.

Direct payments for care

Chapter 1 identified four members of the main sample who made payments towards their primary care arrangements. Two of these payments were made to organisations which existed to provide care and support for people with disabilities.

> Mrs Wright paid over her attendance allowance – £32.95 per week – to the housing association which provided 34 hours of care through the staff of the neighbouring residential home. The fee was determined by the amount of her allowance, rather than by the actual cost of the care, which must have been subsidised by the charity which ran the home.

> Ms Darley paid only £10 per week for her local authority services: a total of 26 hours from a weekday care attendant, a weekend nurse and a home help. The fee was determined by the fact that she was on income support, and was therefore unconnected with the theoretical availability of the attendance allowance.

Both Mrs Wright and Ms Darley received income support and depended entirely on state benefits for their income. Both had quite high incomes by income support standards, receiving mobility allowance as well as the higher rate attendance allowance, while their housing costs were covered by rent rebates. But in both of these cases where formal charges were being levied by organisations (albeit at heavily subsidised rates) all the resources involved in the transfer came from the state system.

Two other 'ordinary' claimants were paying for primary care which they had arranged privately. In both cases, the recipient of the money was already closely tied to the disabled person beforehand.

> Mrs Paxton received 30 hours of care a week from her daughter-in-law, to whom she paid £30 per week. This figure was probably arrived at as an approximation to her attendance allowance of £32.95. At £1 an hour, the daughter-in-law's pay was well below the market rate.

> Mrs Paxton said that, although her daughter-in-law had been reluctant to accept payment, she felt obliged to pay for the care she received:

> > *I've got to pay my daughter-in-law ... I can't expect her to do something for nothing ... She didn't want any payment (but) I said 'I'm getting it from the Government. You take it ... Otherwise I'd have had to pay it from my own money.'*

> Mrs Cox paid exactly her attendance allowance to the friend
> and lodger who cared for her while her husband was at work.
> The arrangement was practical and convenient to both parties,
> since the lodger had retired and was at home most of the day.
> Mrs Cox did not feel she was imposing on her carer ('I could
> not expect him to do it for nothing'); while he benefited from
> the £22 a week extra on top of his pension.

Whereas those paying for care provided by formal agencies had
both been on income support, both of these informal payments were
being made by disabled people who had some resources of their own,
independent of the social security system. Mrs Paxton had a widow's
pension from her husband's employer, and some income from savings
or investments. Mr Cox had been able to retain his full-time
employment while his lodger/friend took his turn at caring.

Moreover both the recipients of these payments had another
income which enabled them to accept a non-economic rate for the job:
Mrs Paxton's son supported his wife and may be considered to have
been helping to finance the arrangement; the Cox's lodger had a
pension of his own.

In both of these cases, therefore, it may have been the attendance
allowance which was paid over, but it looks like the payment could
not have been made if other resources had not been available.

Chapter 1 also identified some people with disabilities who
purchased specific services in addition to their main source of care.
There was one case involving payment to a formal organisation in an
arrangement broadly similar to Mrs Wright's and Ms Darley's.

> The mother of a mentally handicapped young woman spent £10
> for her daughter to spend two nights a week in a short-stay
> hostel, so that she would be prepared for life in a residential
> home when her mother died.

Two elderly couples paid someone they already knew to help with
the housework on a regular basis.

> Mrs Bull paid her daughter £25 out of her £32.95 attendance
> allowance to help her caring husband with the domestic work
> shopping, cleaning, ironing and so on. The attendance
> allowance made this arrangement acceptable for both parties;
> as Mrs Bull said:
>
> > *It's good to have that money because you can get a little
> > bit of help from your family like that ... All right, my*

> *daughter feels awful taking it, but it helps her in a way, and she helps me by doing it.*

Mr and Mrs Dartington gave a friend what they could – 'no set amount' – for a couple of hours help each week with the housework. There was no apparent connection with the attendance allowance or any other particular source of income.

Both of these informal arrangements had much in common with Mrs Paxton's and Mrs Cox's payments to kin and friend respectively. The money paid was not thought of in terms of pounds per hour in the way that would have been appropriate if a stranger had been hired. Both the Bulls and the Dartingtons had an occupational pension to take them above the basic welfare level; though neither couple was well off, this extra may have been just enough to allow them to release some income to pay their supporters. And both of the women who came in to help with the housework thought of their husbands as their principal source of income, and so could afford to provide help without thinking of it as a 'job'.

Two other people were able to pay for non-standard forms of therapy to alleviate the physical problems associated with their disability.

Mr Goodwin purchased two mornings a week of physiotherapy in his own home. It cost £27 a week. In his view it was the attendance allowance (£32.95 a week) which allowed him to do this although he said that he probably could still have afforded the physiotherapy even without the allowance.

A disabled woman purchased a morning a week of yoga tuition in her own home, at a cost of £10 a week. However, as far as she and her husband were concerned, they simply made the £10 available from their weekly budget, without linking it specifically to the attendance allowance.

Mr Goodwin was used as the example of relative affluence earlier in this chapter, and in fact both of these disabled people had high incomes relative to others. Both thought of these services as 'luxuries' which they would have had to dispense with if they had been short of money for basics.

So, among the 29 attendance allowance claimants outside the Bexley scheme, nine turned out to be receiving regular personal services for which they made a weekly payment. Table 3 summarises their arrangements. Other people with disabilities, or their carers, had

Table 3   Payments for care

Primary care, formal services

two did not have a kin carer; they paid formal services for the care which enabled them to remain in the community

Primary care, informal relationships

two paid their attendance allowance to the relative or a close friend who looked after them

Support, formal services

one paid for a weekly overnight stay in a hostel

Support, informal relationships

two paid a relative or friend who helped with the housework

Therapy, formal services

two paid for therapy to alleviate the physical problems associated with their disability

---

paid for services on occasions to help with spring cleaning, to do decorating or other difficult tasks, or to provide cover when the main carer was away or needed a break. But it has not been possible to analyse these irregular transactions in relation to people's incomes.

None of the regular payments exceeded the amount of the claimant's attendance allowance, and several were explicitly based on that benefit. In some cases, the existence of a source of income with that name enabled the payment to be made without the embarrassment which would normally have been involved in money transactions between relatives or between friends.

Nearly one-third of the sample is, perhaps, more than might have expected to have been found paying for care. But most of the nine cases had two things in common which weaken the interpretations that the allowance was widely used for this purpose.

- None of the arrangements for providing household or personal care were seen by the participants to represent anything like a market contract between buyer and supplier. Only the two private therapy sessions were paid for on that basis: in all the other cases, there was a strong suggestion that the payment did not cover the full economic costs of the service, and a presumption that the care would have been provided anyway, with or without the payment. There is no sign of a market here.

51

- With the exception of the two people who made a contribution to the costs of care by altruistic organisations, all of who paid anything for personal services had an occupational pension or a wage which took their incomes above the level of basic social assistance plus attendance allowance. It can be suggested that it is the combination of attendance allowance plus independent income which allowed them to make this payment; if the allowance was added only to basic benefits, it could not be released from basic expenses.

Indirect payments for care

Among the 29 members of the sample of 'ordinary' attendance allowance claimants, just over half reported that a relative had given up work, retired early or taken part-time work in order to be able to care for them.

Reduced or lost earnings represent an opportunity cost to the carer. We have not attempted to calculate these costs in terms of incomes foregone, but they could be substantial. At the extreme, they could consist of a full wage or salary of hundreds of pounds per week. Even those who were able to leave their employment on early retirement terms suffered a loss, which could last for the rest of their life:

> The man who took early retirement at 52 in order to care for his wife was experiencing loss of earnings, partially compensated by his pension, during the period prior to the normal retirement age. He would continue to face a financial loss thereafter because of reduced pension entitlement: his years of service were less than they would have been if he had retired at 65, and his salary was lower than it would have been by the time he reached 65.

These financial costs were borne in the first instance by the carer him or herself, but they could often be shared. Some carers became entitled to social security benefits – the invalid care allowance or income support – when they gave up work, and the social security system may be considered to have met part of the financial costs of care in those instances. In other cases, the carer had previously contributed to a household budget which supported other members of his or her family; to the extent that their joint standard of living declined, the family would have shared the cost of caring. Thus the cost represented by reduced earnings could be spread about in quite complicated ways, though the carers themselves were always among the heaviest losers.

In principle the disabled person could also contribute to this indirect cost of caring, to the extent that his or her income contributed to the standard of living enjoyed by the carer. Incomes were very commonly pooled, and administered by the carer, and it was not possible to pin the flows of income and expenditure down with any precision. In general it seemed that most transfers were in the opposite direction – that carers' income was being used to support the disabled person's expenditure, rather than the other way round. But it might be argued that any specific increase in the disabled person's income might reduce the costs incurred by the carer, and/or improve the whole family's joint standard of living. If so, that element of income could be seen as a contribution to the indirect costs of caring.

There were some indications that the attendance allowance may have had an effect on the supply of care which might suggest that it was an indirect form of payment.

- There were four kin carers who had chosen to work part-time rather than full-time so that they could continue their caring role. Three of them said explicitly that it was the attendance allowance which had made it financially possible for them to reduce their hours of work.

  That is where the attendance allowance comes in handy ... I really needed to work full-time. But that really wasn't ideal, not with Mum, because on a bad day, if I am at work, then Mum has got no choice but to stay in bed the whole day.

- One man who cared for his disabled wife said that it was the attendance allowance (or, rather, the combination of the three benefits received by his wife, including attendance allowance) which had enabled him to retire early and care for his wife.

It was seen at the beginning of the chapter that some people thought of the attendance allowance as a form of contribution to the costs of caring kin. Although the direct evidence is not clear, it could be argued that this indirect form of paying for care might be as important as the more direct payments analysed in the preceding section.

References

1. J. Martin and A. White, *The Financial Circumstances of Disabled Adults Living in Private Households*, HMSO, 1988.

2. P. Thompson, *Short Changed by Disability*, Disablement Income Group, 1990. The figure of £70 is for people in disability severity categories 9 and 10, excluding costs met by the Independent Living Fund.

4 The Bexley Community Care Scheme

The Community Care Scheme was described in the Introduction. Its clients are elderly people suffering from senile dementia, who were at risk of going into residential care. The care manager arranges a team of non-kin carers based on a preliminary assessment of need. We would therefore expect the results to be quite different from those found in the sample of 'ordinary' claimants, most of whose care arrangements had been developed ad hoc by their relatives.

Key carers

In the ordinary sample, we found that 27 disabled people turned to a close relative to take on the main responsibility for their care; the majority of them lived with that relative. Only two were cared for in a more formal arrangement with non-relatives.

Among the nine clients of the Bexley scheme, two lived with a close relative who retained the principal responsibility for care in an arrangement very similar to those found elsewhere. The distinctive feature of the scheme from their point of view was the provision of support.

At the other extreme were two clients who had no contact with any relatives. For them, there was a straight choice between paid-for care at home or in an institution.

Several members of the scheme, however, had children who participated to a greater or lesser extent in the care arrangements, but who were not principal carers. Their contributions varied: some lived nearby and visited almost daily; some contributed to the financial package; all would have expected to be consulted about any major problem. These kin held a general responsibility for ensuring that their mothers or fathers received care, but it was a paid carer who had had taken on much of the immediate responsibility from day to day.

The scheme could be seen, therefore, to provide support for, or an alternative to, a kin carer, as well as offering care at home to the disabled person.

Apart from the two who lived with a close relative, the members of the Bexley sample had a principal carer who was not related to them, in an arrangement almost without parallel in the main sample of people who had not benefited from the scheme. Three examples are described in the boxed text on the next two pages, to illustrate the range of variation. Each case had its own particular characteristics, and it is difficult to generalise on the basis of so small a group. Indeed, the capacity to choose a different solution for each client might be claimed as one of the advantages of the scheme, though it no doubt implies a high administrative cost at the time each arrangement is being set up.

Even among the seven cases, it was possible to identify some patterns of variation:

- Variations in *the role of kin* have already been described.
- Another difference between cases was in *the location of the carer*. In addition to the two close relatives who lived with the disabled person, two of the paid carers lived with their client under a home-sharing arrangement, and were available throughout the night. But the remaining clients lived alone, with their carers coming in from their own homes nearby.
- A third feature of the cases was the *method of recruitment*. Two of the carers were experienced care-workers who helped to look after other people besides the member of our sample; two others had previously worked for the disabled person as a local authority home-help and extended their duties when the new arrangements were required. These four, then, were contacted within the existing community care network; the other three were recruited in the neighbourhood through advertising.

Mrs Cherry – care provided by homesharers

Mrs Cherry suffered from Alzheimer's Disease. She was beginning to wander out in the streets at night, when her daughter who lived nearby, but was too unwell to care for her mother herself, decided that her mother needed a live-in carer. She had the idea that it might be possible to find a family to live with her mother and supervise her at night, in return for free accommodation and a small payment. She contacted the community care scheme because she wanted assistance with drawing up a 'homeshare agreement' covering such matters as bills, shared and private areas of the house, and so on.

She placed an advertisement in the 'jobs vacant' section of the local newspaper and received thirty applications. She interviewed twelve couples, saying that they were all 'quite suitable – any one of them would have done'. Since then, several families have stayed with Mrs Cherry, and only one of them caused any problems. Her daughter described how she felt about this solution:

It's worth every penny and more. If (the family) was paid twice (what they get), it still wouldn't be enough ... My mother improves no end with the children around. It's a lovely atmosphere round there. To do that job, (the family who care for her) are lovely, loving people.

Mrs Aintree – care provided by paid neighbours

Mrs Aintree spent much of the day in bed and was incontinent. The community care scheme became involved while she was in hospital. A meeting was held, involving the manager of the community care scheme, Mrs Aintree's son (who was living away from his mother), a nurse, an occupational therapist and a social worker. It was decided to try to recruit a carer from among Mrs Aintree's immediate neighbours, to enable her to return to live in her home as she wished. A neighbour described how she came to be Mrs Aintree's carer:

A leaflet came through the door and I thought 'I don't mind a couple of hours a week shopping.' It was just something to help a handicapped person.

This 'key carer' then recruited three further members of the care 'team'. Together, they provided 42 hours a week of care and domestic assistance, paid for out of Mrs Aintree's attendance allowance and other income, with subsidies from her son.

Mrs Binney – care provided by home help who extended her duties

Mrs Binney lived alone in a block for elderly people, but her behaviour had been causing uproar among her neighbours. Mrs Binney already had a devoted home help, who wanted to do more. With the agreement of the home help organiser, the home help's role was extended to that of carer, the extra hours of work being paid for out of the benefits obtained through the community care scheme. The home help's daughter also helped out as a carer, and even, on occasion, the home help's husband.

The neighbours were soon reconciled to Mrs Binney's living near them, and some of them popped in to see her with cups of tea. As the community care manager put it:

It's what it ought to be and it very often does happen like that, where the whole family becomes a surrogate family to this old lady and they love it.

In the words of the home help:

I just got roped in and got on with it sort of thing. It's not put me out as such or anything.... It's just worked out that I've got myself that little bit more involved than I intended.

One striking feature of the arrangements was the extent to which many of the non-relatives had developed a 'family' type relationship with the person they looked after. Mrs Cherry's daughter commented on the 'lovely atmosphere' created by the homesharer's own family. Mrs Binney's home-help shared the work with her own daughter, and asked her husband to help out on occasions, in a relationship which the scheme organiser described as a 'surrogate family'. Another carer sometimes invited her 'client' for Sunday dinner. A social worker commented:

(She) is very fond of him but incapable of asking for money ... She has gradually stepped into the daughter role and now makes all decisions and copes with personal care, bills, working and cleaning.

Support for key carers

An important point about the role of the principal carer within the Community Care Scheme was that no-one had to look after a disabled person 24 hours a day, seven days a week. Although at first sight the

Table 4 Care and support for the Bexley clients

Client	Key carer	Relatives	Paid helpers	Social Services	Health services
Mrs Jameson	Daughter	Key carer	Three helpers 14 hrs per week	None	None
Mr Sergeant	Wife	Key carer	Agency 15 hrs, Neighbour 10½ hrs	Home help 12 hrs	Community nurse 10½ hrs, Hospital 2 weeks in 6
Mrs Cherry	Homesharer	Daughter calls in frequently	Two neighbours 2 hrs, Sitters 2 evenings	Meals on wheels	None
Mrs Crawley	Homesharer	Daughter 14 hrs	Helper 10 hrs	None	None
Mrs Pinner	Agency supervisor	Daughter at weekends 4 hrs	Agency workers 32½ hrs	None	None
Mrs Aintree	Neighbour 22 hrs	Son, lives away but visits weekly	Two helpers 18 hrs	None	Nurse 2 hrs
Mrs Binney	Home help with extended role 12 hrs	Daughter lives in West Country	Helper 2 hrs	Day centre 7 hrs, Meals on wheels	Nurse 5 hrs
Mrs Williamson	Neighbour 8 hrs	None	Two helpers 7 hrs	Home help 5 hrs, Lunch club 6 hrs	None
Mr Meredith	Ex-home help 35–40 hrs	None	Two neighbours at weekends 10 hrs	Day centre 7 hrs	Nurse ½ hr Hospital, 1 week in 5

most distinctive feature of the scheme is the assignment of responsibility to a non-kin carer, it is also striking how much help and support the carers received. The same was true whether the leadership lay with a relative or a paid carer: the principal carer did some of the work, and arranged for other people to do some of it. One principal carer was acting as an agency, hiring staff to provide the care, and acting as a supervisor rather than as worker. At the other end of the spectrum, one live-out carer put in a forty hour week, and the live-in carers would have had long periods of duty; but all of these could also rely on other people to take regular turns. No-one was put under the continuous strain accepted by some of the kin carers in the sample of ordinary attendance allowance claimants.

Table 4 summarises the care and support received by each of the nine disabled people in the Bexley sample. Each arrangement was set up ad hoc, depending partly on the availability of kin, as well as on the needs of the individual client. Support came from four separate sources: from members of the disabled person's family; from additional non-kin carers paid directly; from the local authority social services department; and from the local health authority. But while some disabled people benefitted from officially-provided services, others did not.

The five clients whose carers did not live with them received between 26 and 57 hours of care per week. The four live-in carers could not estimate how many hours they put in each week, but they had other forms of help and support totalling between 14 and 47 hours per week. It can be imagined how glad the carers of disabled people who were not members of the scheme would have been to have received support on anything like that scale.

'Teams'

These arrangements whereby a number of different people and organisations combine to deliver care to one person are often referred to as 'packages', although the organisers of the scheme prefer to emphasise the links between their members by calling them 'teams'. Compared with the patchwork of statutory services that some disabled people had received previously, respondents in Bexley often said that the one-to-one cover supported by statutory and paid services provided a much more flexible and satisfactory arrangement:

It's the best because you're buying what you want, when you want it. You're not getting it put on a plate saying 'this is what there is; that is what you've got to have'. That may not suit what you need. And most of the people it doesn't suit their needs. They don't want to be got up at 10 in the morning by a district nurse, because they are used to getting up at seven or eight in the morning ... They don't want to be put to bed at 6.30 at night. They want to stay up and watch Dallas!

It crosses over the rigid lines that have been made by the social services. A home help can only do a, b, c, d. The district nurse will only do the other bit and don't you tread on my patch. It creates atmospheres and you get people wrangling.

Many of these arrangements seemed to work well:

We work together ... It's sticking together and working together that keeps us all sane.

On the other hand, complex schemes involving the coordination of several different carers did not always operate perfectly. Some of the specialist services could not be fitted in at the times which would have been ideal from the carer's point of view:

In the morning I waste time ... I'm hanging around waiting (for the District Nurse) ... I can't get the washing on the go until they've been, because I don't know if there will be any wet sheets.

Because most of the disabled people in this group were very confused, we did not consult them directly, but the constant rotation of faces and voices may have unsettled them, and, perhaps, added to their confusion. There were some signs of irritation with a member of the care team:

The girl she's got at the weekend ... she's very very nice but she's one of these people who tend to patronise old people. It's "is that all right, love, are you sure that's all right?" and of course Mrs W hates that, like a lot of old people do. It's getting on her nerves a bit. (Principal carer.)

And of course the principal carer was not always happy with every member of the team:

Her daughter gets terribly neurotic and worries constantly about her ... she has to be kept at arm's length.

Problems of this sort are probably inevitable when many different people are trying to cope with a situation which was difficult in the first place. None of the care teams in this study had fallen out so seriously for care cover to break down; it can be assumed that if they had, the care manager who had helped to make the arrangements in the first place could have intervened and put things right.

Opinions about the scheme

It was emphasised in the introduction that this exploratory research was *not* set up to perform an evaluation of the Bexley scheme in terms of the content of what was done. We are concerned only with the economic and administrative questions about how it was arranged for a given number of hours care to be delivered; a much more intensive inquiry would be required before judgements could be passed as to whether the right kind of care was being offered, or whether it was the best solution for the client. We can, however, pass on the comments of some of the people who were involved.

The relatives and carers of the nine clients of the Bexley Community Care Scheme whom we interviewed described the situation prior to the involvement of the scheme as being unsatisfactory or distressing for the elderly person concerned. Relatives were often desperate when they first came into contact with the scheme, and in most cases, there was a real possibility that the disabled person would have to go into a residential home or hospital.

The scheme was seen as having made a considerable improvement to the situation of the disabled person. The scheme organisers' skills in obtaining benefits and coordinating services were much admired. Carers and relatives thought the arrangements were flexible, reliable, and designed to meet the particular needs of the elderly person.

Care arrangements were usually developed after an initial assessment of the client's needs, including advice from a clinical psychologist. This often meant that relatives and/or principal carers could be told what to expect of an old person suffering from dementia. Second, it was sometimes possible to include a programme of rehabilitation, rather than simply taking over certain activities. Sometimes it might be decided, for example, that the disabled person should be expected to take responsibility for the shopping and housework themselves, rather than rely on a home help provided by the social services department.

The following account of an old lady's transition from hospital to the community by her key carer illustrates some of the advantages of rehabilitation in the community:

> *I did an assessment visit in the hospital... I said 'Hello, I'm Frances', and started the conversation by saying 'Have you had your lunch?' 'No. Yes.'; 'Well what did you have?' 'No. Yes.' There was no conversation at all...*
>
> *Now she can make a cup of tea for herself and she does her washing up. She gets undressed and into bed and she gets herself up in the morning ... So her whole life has changed and it's opened up again. She's gained confidence ... and she's enjoying it, being at home.*

One of the objectives of keeping elderly people in the community was to ensure that they continued to exercise a degree of responsibility and control over their own lives. One elderly woman was given a budget out of which she was obliged to provide for her homesharer's and her own food and keep:

> *She's got to feel that she's looking after someone ... If you remove him ... she hasn't got a reason to live. (Daughter).*

The same woman had to be retaught how to go out to the shops. Her daughter describes her first trip on her own:

> *We gave her her trolley and her purse and said 'away you go'. I drove round Bexleyheath shadowing her. People must have thought I was crazy. I was hiding in shop doorways. She was absolutely over the moon, she was brilliant. She was dodging about in shops and beaming from ear to ear. It was a joy to see her.*

Another group of people affected by the Bexley arrangements consisted of the clients' relatives. Some relatives continued to take a direct part in care management, while others played a background role. Either way, they found their responsibilities stressful, particularly if they were elderly or unwell themselves. Many said that, without the help of the scheme, they did not know how they would have coped:

> *I would have had a complete nervous breakdown ... I just ... thank God that I've got a job that pays me enough money that I can buy in care. (Daughter of woman suffering from dementia.)*

Relatives often spoke in glowing terms of the carers who took on so much responsibility for the elderly people with disabilities. One said 'I trust her implicitly', another, 'I can't speak too highly of her'. Several relatives spoke of the reliability of the care that was provided; for example, some carers arranged cover over Christmas and other public holidays.

There could, on the other hand, be tensions in the relationships between kin and paid carers. One daughter described her difficulties in transferring responsibility to a stranger:

> *I can't let go of Mum now, because if there is anything wrong I want to deal with it. I can't get used to sending notes to Jill saying so and so ... I keep being told that Jill is responsible for mother, not me.*

In other cases, the non-kin carer felt that she was in conflict with her client's next of kin:

> *The daughter would love desperately for her to be in a home, so it's a peace-keeping job the whole time with her ... The least little thing upsets her.*

The third group of people whose interests have to be considered are the workers – especially those who had taken on the responsibility of being a key carer. More detailed studies of the motivations and rewards of paid carers have been carried out by Diana Leat.[1] Most of the non-kin carers who were interviewed for our own research were happy with their work. For some of them, it provided an good opportunity for part-time employment close to home, which could be combined with their own domestic responsibilities. Several felt 'involved' in their work in a way which was not possible in many low-skill occupations.

> *There are lots of lonely old people and there's lots of people that would like to help. But they can't get together ... There are people that this little job is ideal for. They don't want to earn a fortune. They don't want to pay tax on anything, but they could do with a few bob extra. (Paid neighbour caring for elderly lady.)*

> *It's giving people a job and a home ... It's a lovely idea. (Daughter of woman with a homeshare arrangement.)*

The scheme aimed to achieve a one-to-one relationship between the disabled person and their carer as a 'surrogate daughter'. The scheme supported the key carer with advice, a newsletter, information about carers' groups they could join, courses on medical problems such as dementia, and sometimes counselling. Carers were encouraged to gain the confidence to take decisions about the different kinds of needs of the person they are caring for. 'The whole ethos of the scheme', according to its manager, is to ensure that carers become 'the boss of their own situation'.

But some carers said that the level of responsibility for the elderly person they cared for weighed heavily on them. One felt that this was affecting her own family:

> *If I was a nurse with geriatric patients in a hospital, I would walk away from it to my own family. But I don't ... I do get tired sometimes because I get calls out during the night as well. That affects my husband because he comes with me at night. He won't let me go up there alone ... Ray is like a Dad to us all now. He spends Christmas with us ... It's not a situation I would get into again, but as I've got into it, I can't walk away from it. You accept it, don't you, and make the best of it.*

One woman reflected the potential problems for carer's families when she pointed out that it was only acceptable to her now that she was a widow – 'he wouldn't like me being called on any minute of the day'.

Most carers felt under considerable moral pressure to do what was asked for or needed by the person they cared for. One daughter said that her mother's carer 'does an awful lot above and beyond what she's paid for', and several other relatives and carers echoed these words. One woman had previously worked as a home help for the person she cared for, and it was discovered when she came onto the community care scheme that she had been cooking meals for the disabled person, but concealing this from the home help organiser because it was against the rules.

Many of the informal carers carried out both domestic and 'nursing' tasks (such as bathing the elderly person and changing light dressings and incontinence pads), yet they had received no 'nursing' training. One carer, for example, had not spotted the symptoms when the person she was caring for developed a bladder infection which required hospital treatment: she felt that there ought to have been weekly check-ups from a qualified person, such as a nurse, in addition to the care she provided.

If carers had taken on responsibility for personal finances, there were potential risks of impropriety on either side. One carer, concerned to protect herself against the possibility that she might in the future be accused of theft or misappropriation of funds, took the trouble to formalise her financial responsibility through a solicitor. Another carer had been left the disabled person's house in his will, and the community care manager worried that the carer might be open to exploitation by her client.

Some of the elderly people depended on quite complicated care arrangements, and this could cause problems of coordination. One carer had in effect three bosses: the home help organiser, the community care manager and the elderly person she cared for. The different members of the care team needed to work together, or there could be problems.

Carers could also suffer as a result of the informality of their employment contract. Their hourly earnings at the time when the research was carried out were quite low – around £3.50 per hour – although against this has to be set the probability that many of them did not have to pay any tax. More important, perhaps, the carers were not afforded the usual protections of employment legislation such as protection from unfair dismissal, rights to holidays and sick leave, and so on. Carers would have had no redress, for example, if they had injured their back while lifting the person they were caring for, since they were not covered by health and safety legislation. Some were insured against this sort of risk, but others were not.

Paying the costs

Although several of the 'ordinary' attendance allowance claimants were paying for care in some way or another, they were buying relatively small quantities, or obtaining it at preferential or non-market rates. None of them was paying more than the amount of their attendance allowance. Among the members of the Bexley community care scheme, on the other hand, we have seen that much larger amounts of outside care were being provided; and most of it was paid for at a rate of between £3 and £4 per hour – about the average for part-time female workers. The cost of this care was therefore much higher.

Table 5 itemises the cash cost of the services paid for by each of the nine respondents. The minimum cost was £50 per week – more than twice the amount of the attendance allowance claimed by the

Table 5 Costs of paid care for Bexley clients; and sources of income

	Mrs Jameson	Mr Sergeant	Mrs Cherry	Mrs Crawley	Mrs Pinner	Mrs Aintree	Mrs Binney	Mrs Williamson	Mr Meredith
Cost of care	£50	£85	£130	£75	£85	£130	£50	£70	£135
'Available' income									
Attendance allowance	£20	£30	£30	£30	£20	£20	£20	£20	£30
Domestic assistance addition	£20	–	£60	£35	£75	–	£30	£25	–
Private pension	–	£30	–	–	–	£10	–	–	£70
Earnings of wife	–	£25	–	–	–	–	–	–	–
Income from savings	–	–	–	–	–	–	–	£5	£50
Charity	–	–	£10	£10	–	–	–	–	–
Contribution from son/daughter	£20	–	£20	–	–	£85	–	–	–
Total	£60	£85	£120	£75	£95	£115	£50	£50	£150
Surplus of available income	+£10	=	-£10	=	+£10	-£15	=	-£20	+£15

people concerned. The average was £90. Three claimants were spending £130 or £135 per week – not far short of £20 per day. These figures refer only to the cash costs met directly: services given for free by relatives or friends are not counted; nor those provided without charge by the social services or the NHS; services provided at subsidised rates are counted at the rate charged, not at full cost. Two of the disabled people contributed an implicit payment to their carers in the form of rent-free accommodation, but again this is not counted.

The same table shows the 'available' income of each person. It is assumed that the basic social security benefits (state pension, supplementary benefit/income support and housing benefit) are intended to meet people's basic living costs, but that any other sources of income might be considered to be 'available' to be spent on other things, such as care. (The mobility allowance is not counted since it is supposed to be earmarked for transport costs.) It was not always possible to obtain exact amounts, and one or two of the figures have been inferred on the basis of indirect evidence. All the figures (including the attendance allowance) have been rounded to the nearest £5 to indicate that the calculations are not precise.

In spite of some inaccuracies, the table shows clearly that another source of income was always required in order to meet the costs of care in the community.

- In two cases, the claimants themselves had sufficient resources to meet the costs of care. Mr Meredith had a pension from his former employer, and a sizeable nest-egg of savings, from which he was able to pay £135 for care and still have a little left over for everyday expenditure. Mr Sergeant had a smaller pension, but his wife's earnings from part-time work were also available. In both cases the attendance allowance plus their own resources were sufficient to cover the costs, although buying in care transformed what could have been a comfortable standard of living to near-poverty.

- In one case, most of the additional income was provided by the disabled person's family. Mrs Aintree's son worked in a bank and felt he could afford to support his mother in this way, though he could not have managed the full costs of residential care.

- In the remaining six cases, the costs of care in excess of the attendance allowance were met, or largely met, by the

Department of Social Security through the domestic assistance addition to supplementary benefit. Two of the budgets also included a subsidy from daughters; two of them included small but regular contributions from charities.

The interviews with Bexley claimants were undertaken at just about the time when supplementary benefit was being replaced by income support. Under the former scheme, claimants were entitled to additional benefit to pay for domestic assistance, if this was provided privately, not by the local authority. Very few of these additions were paid, but they were clearly vital to the Bexley scheme; among these nine claimants, the domestic assistance addition contributed as much to the costs of care as the attendance allowance.

The domestic assistance addition was abolished in April 1988, and replaced by income support disability premiums which would not have provided anything like so much. The people who were already claiming the addition would not have lost it all immediately, because their benefit was maintained in cash terms by transitional protection. The more direct replacement for the domestic assistance addition has been the Independent Living Fund. We understand that several members of the Bexley scheme have successfully applied to the Fund for support.

In the sample of disabled people who were not members of the Bexley scheme, it was suggested that the attendance allowance was not spent on care unless there was some other source of income which released it. Among the Bexley sample the conclusion is reinforced: the attendance allowance on its own was nowhere near enough to support a viable package of care. On the other hand it always made an important contribution. The scheme relied on the attendance allowance plus... In three cases the plus came from the client and/or the family; in six, from the domestic assistance addition.

It has already been said that the scheme's organisers are important: first, to assess the needs of each disabled person; and second to help put together a team of workers. A third role, almost as important as the other two, is to assemble the financial resources.

In several cases, the attendance allowance had been applied for and obtained by the scheme organisers on behalf of their clients, expressly for the purpose of paying for care. The scheme manager admitted that it would be difficult to persuade people who had been receiving attendance allowance for some time to consider using that money to start paying for care. However those who had not previously received the allowance, did find it acceptable to spend the money in this way.

> *She is one of the people who have had a hard life, like they all did then, and they like their bit of money ... She would never pay for help herself (before she received the attendance allowance) even if she could afford it. (Paid neighbour caring for woman suffering from dementia.)*

> *This money is hers ... She knows she is paying her way. She doesn't want hand-outs from the family ... She's worked all her life and she's earned it. (Daughter of woman suffering from dementia.)*

In addition to the attendance allowance, the scheme's manager had shown considerable ingenuity in negotiating a domestic assistance addition for so many people, and has continued to take the same line with the Independent Living Fund. As she said:

> *There's always enough money if you're prepared to really study to get it. But you've got to go all out to get it.*

References

1. D. Leat, *Paying for Care*, PSI, 1987; *For Love and Money*, JRMT, forthcoming, 1990.

5 Conclusions about social security and paid care

The Bexley Community Care Scheme
We have been looking for a link between the attendance allowance and the costs of caring through a comparison of the experiences of two groups of people – 'ordinary' attendance allowance claimants, and the members of a special scheme in which the allowance is used directly to pay for care. We will review the findings about that scheme, before going on to draw conclusions about the impact of the allowance on the broader group of claimants.

Family circumstances
In the sample of attendance allowance claimants who were not members of the Bexley scheme, almost everyone was looked after by a close relative. It seemed likely that the majority of people with severe disabilities who did not have a kin carer had been obliged to take a place in a residential home. In the Bexley sample, members of the family often participated in the design of the care arrangements, and some of them took an active part in providing day to day care. But the majority of these relatives had assigned the lead role to paid carers.

A minority of the Bexley clients appeared to have no support from any relatives, and they were dependent on whatever arrangements could be made for them by the social services department or other agencies.

It is highly likely that members of this latter group would have been taken into a home if a community care arrangement had not been set up. For those with family support, it is not clear how many would have gone into residential care, and how many would have been taken on full-time by a daughter or son.

Care teams
Each client of the Bexley scheme had a team of carers arranged in consultation between representatives of the family, social services, health services and voluntary organisations, as appropriate. A 'key carer' was always found. Two relatives remained the key carer, but benefited from support services. Other key carers included:

- a family who lived in the client's home, rent-free, in return for providing care;
- a home help who was asked to take on responsibility for care in addition to the housework she had already been doing for many years;
- a neighbour who was recruited through an advertisement;
- an employee of a commercial agency.

The main carer's own commitment ranged from a few hours to a full working week. But none had the 168-hour responsibility experienced by some kin carers outside the scheme. Each was supported by a regular rota of other services including domiciliary nurses, home-helps, day centres, respite care or sitters. The total added up to between 14 and 58 hours per week. Few of the carers in the sample of 29 'ordinary' attendance allowance claimants obtained anything like as much help from outside sources.

Resources
The care arranged for the clients of the Bexley scheme was paid for from a variety of sources, and it was often difficult to pin down exactly how much had been contributed by each.

Many of the disabled people benefited from caring services provided free, or at reduced cost, by the health authority or the local authority social services department. Some of them received fairly regular help from daughters, sons or other kin; a few of them were assisted on a voluntary basis by friends and neighbours. Some of the paid carers did more than they were contracted to do. In all these cases it was the provider of the care who was paying part or all of its cost, although only in the case of formal services would it be possible to assign a realistic money value to the contribution.

In spite of these hidden subsidies, the cash costs of the care arrangements ranged from £50 to £135 per week; between twice and four times the amount provided by the attendance allowance.

In two-thirds of the cases, the allowance had been topped up by a domestic assistance addition to supplementary benefit – an allowance to cover the cost of privately provided home helps which never became widely used. The smallest of these additions was as much as that claimant's attendance allowance; the largest, three times the allowance.

The domestic assistance addition was abolished in April 1988. Its nearest equivalent is the new Independent Living Fund, a charitable organisation financed by the government but administered by the Disablement Income Group. It is understood that several Bexley clients have successfully applied to the ILF over the past two years; given the importance of the domestic assistance addition, the scheme might not have been able to continue without this substitute.

One client relied on her son to meet the majority of her expenses. Two others had regular financial help from their family which met some of the costs of care, but these contributions were less important than their domestic assistance addition.

Only two clients had resources which, combined with their attendance allowance, could meet the costs of care without further help from outside the household. But their expenditure on care, over and above the attendance allowance, reduced the income which would otherwise have been available to these relatively prosperous pensioners; in one case, down to the basic level of living experienced by supplementary benefit/income support claimants. In the end, they were little or no better off than the poorer claimants who had to rely on the domestic assistance addition.

Another resource provided by two of the disabled people was their house, where their carers lived rent free.

So the attendance allowance and basic benefits were not, on their own, enough to allow people to pay for a package of care. It required the allowance *plus* some other major source. It nevertheless represented an important contribution towards the costs of care.

Although the community care scheme's aim is to provide better care for clients and/or relief from the burden of care for relatives, there are economic gains to be taken into account, as well as costs. The gainers are the people or organisations who would have borne the direct or indirect costs of care in the absence of the scheme: relatives, statutory service agencies and the Department of Social Security.

Advantages

All of those associated with the Bexley community care scheme seemed to be pleased with the result.

The prime advantages were seen to be to the clients themselves. Residential care was perceived as an impersonal environment within which disabled people were looked after too much or too little: either way, it led to rapid decline. The home care arrangements were based on individual assessment, providing sufficient care and protection, but at the same time stimulating the client to make as much use of his or her faculties as possible.

Another potential advantage lay in the variety of types of service put together to meet particular needs, instead of selecting from the range of standard services provided by existing agencies.

Some respondents also thought that paying for care provided disabled people with a greater degree of independence than if they relied on the goodwill of their relations, and greater control than if they relied mainly on statutory services.

The scheme was also valued by relatives on their own behalf. They were relieved of the difficult choice between looking after their elderly kin themselves, and 'putting them in a home'.

Some paid carers had not previously found a job which fitted in with their own domestic commitments, and were glad of the employment opportunity provided by the scheme.

Drawbacks

The research was not designed to evaluate the effectiveness of the care provided through the scheme. In principle, it might be argued that the cover might have been less than the client needed. But no-one we spoke to mentioned any problems of that sort.

Some of the care arrangements were largely financed from the personal incomes of the clients or their families. The cost represents a disadvantage to them if the alternative might have been care provided free. All of the members of the scheme had committed their attendance allowance to pay for care, so it was not available for the basic goods and services which most other claimants chose to spend it on.

Some of the potential disadvantages were concerned with the people who were employed as 'carers'. They were taking on a heavy burden not only of work but also of responsibility, in return for modest wages and the poor conditions of service typical of ad hoc employees. While some of them achieved a welcome degree of autonomy, others were not clear who they answered to.

Assessment
There is little doubt that the clients of the Bexley scheme, and their relatives, preferred it to residential care. It was also cheaper. For those whose adult children might have provided care, the benefits of the scheme are at least as important to the family, as to the client him or herself.

Compared with the services available to 'ordinary' people with serious disabilities, clients of the scheme have four advantages:
- the scheme's core staff: a clinical psychologist to assess their particular needs, and a care manager to coordinate services and claim benefits;
- benefit income specifically aimed at care expenditure;
- care services secured in the open market; and
- (in some cases) a significant input of support services provided by formal agencies.

It is unlikely that care arrangements could be built without the combination of these, and it is therefore difficult to decide which are the crucial ingredients.

The Bexley scheme has emerged both to cope with and to exploit the particular combination of public programmes which happens to exist at a particular time. It is important to analyse its components:

The objective: is to enable people suffering from senile dementia to be cared for in their own homes, without placing excessive strain on their daughters or other kin.

The strategy: is to hire people in the open market to play roles which would otherwise be taken by relatives and/or the employees of social services departments.

The tactics: are to obtain resources wherever they can be found – from statutory services, social security benefits, the client or the family.

There is wide agreement about the desirability of the community care objective. The Bexley strategy is one of the options for delivering care which will have to be considered in the development of post-Griffiths[1] care management; it is possible that some local authorities, or perhaps all local authorities, might follow the Bexley example of hiring individual carers. But the scheme could not be replicated on a larger scale without a clearer set of rules about resourcing. The ad hoc tactics only highlight the current division of responsibilities between different national and local government agencies, between the public and the private sectors, and between formal organisations and the family.

'Ordinary' claimants

Most of this report has concentrated on the attendance allowance claimants who were not members of the Bexley scheme. Although there were only 29 of them, selected from two small areas of London, they are our only guide at this stage to the circumstances and behaviour of the majority of attendance allowance claimants up and down the country. Further research is in progress, at PSI and elsewhere, which will provide a more complete assessment.

Spending the attendance allowance

The great majority of them were not spending their allowance on care – certainly not in any direct sense. Unlike the mobility allowance, which was often allocated specifically to meet the costs of transport, the attendance allowance was usually added to general income; indeed, it was often paid by the DSS in a combined order book including their pension, invalidity benefit or income support. So people could not directly distinguish between it and their other sources of income when they described their expenditure.

One theory is that the attendance allowance was originally designed to (help) meet the direct costs of 'attendance'; another is that it was designed to contribute to the higher cost of living faced by people with disabilities, of which payment for care was only a part. Whatever the underlying intention, there is no doubt that claimants are entitled to spend it as they like, with neither a legal nor a moral obligation to allocate it to certain approved purposes.

Most people described some aspect of their household budget which was affected by their disability – extra heating, laundry, diet, travel costs and so on. We did not attempt to measure the total amounts involved. Two other studies have produced inconsistent estimates. Severely disabled people taking part in OPCS's large scale survey reported that they were spending around £11 per week on extra expenses – about half the lower rate of attendance allowance.[2] A small sample interviewed by the Disablement Income Group averaged £70 per week – twice the higher rate of the attendance allowance.[3] Many claimants and carers said that they spent the attendance allowance on these extra basic costs, though few had a very clear conception of exactly what difference the benefit had made, or how the additional money was allocated.

Other people, though, were confident that they would have met the essential extra costs of disability anyway – that was what they meant by the word 'essential'. But the costs placed a heavy strain on basic budgets, so the attendance allowance provided the element of discretionary income to spend on the modest luxuries which made life tolerable.

Paying for care

Either way, the attendance allowance was seen by most claimants as a component of their general income, aimed at maintaining or improving their standard of living, rather than as a direct contribution to the costs of caring. There was another group, however, who paid for some care. Among the 29 in our sample:

Primary care, formal services
- two did not have a kin carer; they paid formal services for the care which enabled them to remain in the community;

Primary care, informal relationships
- two paid their attendance allowance to the relative or a close friend who looked after them;

Support, formal services
- one paid for a weekly overnight stay in a hostel;

Support, informal relationships
- two paid a relative or friend who helped with the housework;

Therapy, formal services
- two paid for therapy to alleviate the physical problems associated with their disability.

The cash cost of these arrangements ranged between £10 and £30 per week (compared with between £50 and £135 in the Bexley scheme). Only two – the therapy sessions – were paid for at the full rate in a transaction which reflected the influences of supply and demand observed in most markets. All the other seven 'charged' well below the full cost of their services; it is not unlikely that they would have continued their side of the arrangement even if the payment had stopped.

- The formal services were organisations committed to service provision, which derived most of their funds from other sources. For them, charging was probably seen as a way of maximising the number of people who could be helped out of a restricted budget.
- The other carers and helpers were relatives or friends who were not doing it for the money. Payment had generally been offered, rather than asked for, and was seen by both sides as a token in recognition of the kindness provided, rather than as an economic exchange.

Some carers and helpers were paid the exact amount of the claimant's attendance allowance, and the name of the benefit helped to legitimise the payments which might otherwise have been a source of embarrassment. In other cases, it was not the attendance allowance as such which was being used to pay for care, though it may have been the allowance which enabled the payment to be made. On the other hand most of the people with disabilities who paid for services had other sources of income, as well as basic benefits, and it can be argued that the attendance allowance on its own would not have left people with enough money to divert from basic needs for this purpose.

Financial support for unpaid carers

Several carers had suffered a substantial loss of income when they took on their responsibilities, and this represents a 'cost of caring' just as real as the cash cost involved in paying a carer. One possibility was that the resources of the disabled person, including the attendance allowance, were contributing some financial support to the carer – at least to the extent of reducing the carer's losses. This might be seen as an indirect form of 'payment'. Another way of looking at it would be to ask if the existence of the benefit helped to establish the financial viability of an arrangement in which a relative gave up work, or incurred other costs, in order to provide care.

The issue is complicated by the fact that there are other social security benefits which carers can claim in their own right – the invalid care allowance and income support. The attendance allowance is important in triggering carers' entitlement to the invalid care allowance; but the attendance allowance itself is intended to meet the needs of the dependant, not the carer. If, on the other hand, a share of the attendance allowance was sufficient to persuade someone to care who otherwise would not have done, that might be seen as a legitimate use of the dependant's income.

Certainly several claimants and carers thought of the attendance allowance in that light – as a form of payment to the carer to take on a job which would have cost the state much more to meet directly.

While the question is easy to discuss in principle, it is difficult to analyse in practice. Most carers lived in the same house as the disabled person, and the housekeeping was run jointly. With all income going into a common budget, it was not possible to work out which members of the household had the use of which money. In some households the carer had a higher income, and was clearly contributing to the support of the disabled person. This was not very common, though, and in most households it would not have made much difference whether income had been pooled or kept separately.

People usually discussed the process by which they became carers without reference to financial considerations. If money was mentioned at all, it was usually to point out the costs. Nevertheless some people mentioned that it was their disabled relative's attendance allowance which had enabled them to reduce their hours of work, or to take early retirement, and so had contributed to the costs of caring.

The prospects for paid care

Although several members of the sample of 'ordinary' claimants were using their attendance allowance to meet part of the cost of their care, not one of them had adopted the Bexley solution of paying someone to look after them as a form of employment in direct competition with other jobs. No doubt there are cases somewhere in Britain where this has happened without the support of a scheme such as the one in Bexley, but it is certainly not a common feature of care in the community. The OPCS survey of people with disabilities[2] reported that nearly one fifth of the most severely disabled adults were paying extra for 'home services', and that the average amount spent on these

79

was £11. But most of these payments were probably contributions towards the costs of home helps provided at subsidised rates by social services departments. Only one in twenty reported 'private domestic help', and one in forty 'private nursing help'.[4]

This form of care has not developed naturally, but it is worth asking whether it would be a good thing to encourage it to grow. There is no doubt of its popularity among the small group of people in Bexley who have tried it, and that is a good enough reason for taking the idea further.

Substitutes or help for kin carers

Some disabled people have no relative who could care for them, so a paid carer in the community would be the only alternative to an institution. At the other end of the spectrum, there are some degrees of kinship in which the assumption of caring responsibilities is so automatic that the question of a substitute scarcely arises.[5] In between there are many people with disabilities who have two or three relatives – probably daughters or sons – who might care for them themselves, but who would be happy to let someone else do it if appropriate arrangements could be made. Several of the Bexley clients were members of this intermediate group in which a paid carer had taken over from a daughter or son. Depending on what would have happened in the absence of the scheme, it could be argued that the daughters and sons were the principal beneficiaries. Some of them were contributing to the cost.

The cost of full substitute care, however, was commonly £100 per week or more, even though free and subsidised services were often available as well. This is undoubtedly cheaper than residential care, but it is unlikely that public resources would normally be found to pay for care if a relative might provide it for free. There is the prospect of a game of chicken between the state and the family in which each threatens to abandon the disabled person in an attempt to blackmail the other to accept the responsibility; there is little doubt that the state would usually win this game with ease.

It is not necessary to think in terms of a stark choice between a kin carer and a paid carer. One of the striking things about the Bexley care arrangements was that no paid carer was expected to deliver the 168 hours per week of unremitting supervision which some of the carers in the main sample had to provide. It is unlikely that anyone would have been found to take on so great a burden, even for ready money. All the key carers in Bexley had support from paid helpers, or from formal services, or both. If kin carers had had anything like as much help, their problems would have been reduced at a stroke. Few enjoyed substantial regular assistance from official services, perhaps because the latter concentrated their resources on people without a family to look after them. Most of them had no paid helpers either. But the idea of hired help for kin carers might be more successful than the suggestion that paid carers should take over from relatives altogether.

Sources of money

The higher rate of attendance allowance would scarcely stretch to as much as two hours per day, even at the low wage rates available to part-time female workers. This would be little enough support for a 24 hour carer, though it would no doubt be welcome. But carers running household budgets consisting just of basic benefits and the attendance allowance did not feel able to divert money from basic necessities to pay for services. One reason for this was the extra expenditure on such things as heating, laundry and so on which were required to maintain the health and comfort of the disabled person. Whatever the reason, people who depended on social security benefits for all or most of their income felt too poor to spend money on services which, when it came to it, they could undertake themselves.

Payment for care out of their own resources became a possibility only if they had other sources of income to take them above the basic benefit line. Such sources might be earnings, an occupational or private pension, or, perhaps, support from a member of the family. People with these extra resources might be in a position to pay for care, though they could impoverish themselves in the process.

One or two relatives of Bexley clients were conscious that their earnings enabled them to pay for care which they might otherwise have had to provide directly. Only one of the carers of 'ordinary' claimants was using his earnings to pay for support. But in general the idea of paying a carer or helper in order to enable the responsible relative to remain in employment was not well developed.

The care arranged under the Bexley community care scheme depended heavily on the old domestic assistance addition, and now on the Independent Living Fund. Since these sources were directly linked to the provision of care and/or support, there was no question of diverting money out of the limited budgets of the disabled people themselves. The costs were genuinely borne by the Department of Social Security. On the other hand a benefit provided on the condition that it should be spent in a particular way limits the independence which might be considered one of the advantages of the attendance allowance. In effect the DSS is saying 'you must spend the money on care, even though you might prefer to spend it on electricity.'[6]

The DSS supports care costs in another way, by providing the invalid care allowance and/or income support to people who are unable to combine work with caring. Not everyone is entitled, and the income on offer is scarcely attractive, but the rules of entitlement can nevertheless provide more support for unpaid carers than for services.

The new disability allowance which the government announced at the beginning of 1990 will incorporate the current attendance allowance with very little modification.[7] A new, lower, level of benefit will be available to people with disabilities not quite severe enough to qualify for the attendance allowance. The government was not specific about what either payment was intended to cover, referring in general terms to 'needs'. If the attendance allowance was not sufficient to allow people to pay for care, it must be assumed that the new allowance of £10 will have even less effect. One of the disappointments of the twin white papers on community care[8] and disability benefits is the absence of any direct consideration of the role of benefits in promoting care, in either policy.

Care management

The government is determined that care costs should not be seen as a social security responsibility. That is why the charges for residential homes currently met by income support are being transferred to social services departments under the 'Griffiths' arrangements.[1] Similarly, the DSS hived off the Independent Living Fund to a charity, rather than ask its local office staff to make judgements about disabled people's needs for domestic assistance. The question arises whether support for paid carers might not be sought from local authority social services departments. Hitherto they have usually provided home helps, care attendants and other services directly, using their own employees. After 1991 their primary role will be to provide the resources and the case managers to ensure that care is provided, without necessarily supplying the services themselves. They might decide to spend some of the budget allocated to each client on paid care – that is someone recruited directly to work for the particular client, rather than an employee of a care-providing organisation.

Those disabled people and relatives who had experience of paid care, or had thought about it, liked the flexibility of the arrangement. Directly-hired carers and helpers were thought to be more responsive to the consumer's needs and preferences than the staff of a larger organisation would be. This advantage might be reduced if the paid carer was hired by the social services department, using its own money; at least partial control would revert to the bureaucracy; the carer would be uncertain whether her employer was the disabled person or the social services department, and might feel answerable to neither.[9] One option might be for the social worker to allocate a sum of money to be spent on care, but to leave the client or the family to hire and supervise the carer. That is how the Independent Living Fund operates.

On the other hand, one of the main lessons to be learned from a comparison between the Bexley clients and 'ordinary' attendance allowance claimants is that there is no longer a natural market in which personal service is exchanged for wages. Several members of the main sample discussed the question of paid care as a mere hypothesis: if they wanted help of this sort, they would have had no idea how to obtain it. The market did not operate at all until the Bexley scheme was set up to act as a broker. The scheme could also act as a regulator: protecting vulnerable clients against the obvious risks of poor service and/or exploitation; ensuring that the carers themselves were properly paid and well-treated. It may be concluded that paid care in the community is not viable without care management. That is precisely the role that the new social services departments will be in a position to adopt.

Any discussion of future development of paid care will, however, have to be explicit about the source of the money. The attendance allowance currently makes a contribution, but is insufficient on its own. The social services department will have a budget, but it will be under immediate pressure to target resources on people who have no other means of meeting their needs. This will tend to be disabled people with no independent income and no kin. There is therefore the prospect that care and support will be subject to a triple or quadruple test: of the disabled person's needs; of his or her income; of the availability of kin as carers; and perhaps of the incomes of kin. Relatives will still be under pressure to accept the duty of care unaided.

References

1. Sir R. Griffiths, *Community Care: agenda for action*, HMSO, 1988.

2. J. Martin and A. White, *The Financial Circumstances of Disabled Adults Living in Private Households*, HMSO, 1988.

3. P. Thompson, *Short-changed by Disability*, Disablement Income Group, 1990

4. J. Martin, A. White, H. Meltzer, *Disabled adults: services, transport and employment*, HMSO, 1989.

5. See, for example, H. Qureshi and A. Walker, *The Caring Relationship*, Macmillan, 1989; and J. Finch, *Family Obligation and Social Change*, Polity Press, 1989.

6. For a general discussion of some of these issues see R. Berthoud, 'Using benefits to pay for care at home' in S. Baldwin, G. Parker and R. Walker (eds), *Social Security and Community Care*, Avebury, 1988.

7. Department of Social Security, *The Way Ahead: benefits for disabled people*, HMSO, 1990.

8. Department of Health and Social Security, *Caring for People*, HMSO, 1989.

9. See D. Leat *Paying for Care*, PSI, 1987; *For Love and Money*, JRMT, forthcoming, 1990.